Language
Crafted

A LINGUISTIC
THEORY OF
POETIC SYNTAX

Language

Crafted

Timothy R. Austin

Indiana University Press | Bloomington

Library of Congress Cataloging in Publication Data

Austin, Timothy R., 1952–
    Language crafted.

    Bibliography: p.
    Includes indexes.
        1. Criticism.   2. Style, Literary.   I. Title.
PN81.A86   1984   801'.95   83-48933
ISBN 0-253-33197-8
1 2 3 4 5 88 87 86 85 84

This book was brought to publication with the aid of a grant from the Andrew W. Mellon Foundation.

For Shena, Jenny, and Katie

Contents

Acknowledgments

This book has resulted from many years of cooperation with and encouragement from teachers, colleagues, and students at the University of Massachusetts, Amherst, and at Loyola University of Chicago. Naming names is a dangerous business; nevertheless the debts I owe to certain individuals demand explicit acknowledgment. I must trust that those whom I may inadvertently omit will attribute the error to my infamously faulty memory rather than to any underestimation of their kindness.

It was in Donald C. Freeman's graduate seminar at the University of Massachusetts that I first understood where my linguistic and literary studies might intersect. Since then, I have been steadily encouraged by him, first as a teacher and then as a colleague, to refine and improve my theory of poetic syntax. To him and to his wife, Margaret, go thanks for friendship, trust, and intermittent hospitality. S. Jay Keyser taught me a great deal about composing an argument, especially that the way one says something may be at least as important as what one says. He also had innumerable bright ideas about how to say things better. Much of whatever expository strength resides in this study should be attributed to his tutelage, and to the more detailed advice of his colleague in journal editing, E. L. Epstein. Since our days in graduate school, Steven Lapointe and Muffy Siegel have always been more than willing to read carefully and to comment thoughtfully. It has been their continued interest that has repeatedly renewed my own conviction that theoretical linguists might benefit as much from my work as would students of literature. Steven in particular has read much of my material in early draft form with an eagle eye and has never failed to pinpoint its shortcomings without in any way discouraging me. I have similarly benefited from the tough-minded and uncompromising criticism of Richard Cureton, whose dissertation I warmly recommend as probably the best work in syntactic stylistics of recent years.

I am happy to acknowledge certain specific acts of generosity in connection with the preparation of this text itself. Jim Gee was kind enough to send me a copy of a textbook manuscript he has been working on. The staff of the Data Center on the Lake Shore Campus of Loyola University of Chicago played the role of midwife to the typescript of this volume, replacing as a group the typist I was grateful not to need. David Gabrovich in particular accepted with great equanimity the early bunglings and later frustrations of a computer neophyte.

Members of my family have helped me in ways too numerous to detail in full. My parents not only accepted my decision to pursue graduate studies in linguistics in the United States at a time when that may have seemed a risky career choice, but have since offered tireless encouragement with the book itself. Both read early drafts of the text with gratifying (if predictable) enthusiasm and offered many suggestions along the way. My parents-in-law, too, have tolerated a family in exile with great generosity. The hospitality of both families during the summer of 1983 made possible a thorough and leisurely revision of the final typescript.

Even they, however, did not have to live with this book, or with me, during the long years of its gestation. The dedication of this volume is a rather weak attempt to reflect the gratitude I feel toward those who did: my wife, Shena, and daughters, Jenny and Katie, who will be as grateful, I am sure, to see this study in print as they have been patient in awaiting its completion.

If I am less fearful of omitting acknowledgment of my financial indebtednesses, this in no way diminishes the sincerity of my thanks to those who have supported my work. The University of Massachusetts awarded a Graduate Dissertation Fellowship to smooth my way while I completed work on the first draft of some of the material this book contains. Loyola University of Chicago later funded two Summer Research Grants and a one-semester leave of absence to facilitate my work at particularly crucial stages. In addition, I had the good fortune to attend classes with E. D. Hirsch and to participate in the other activities of the 1981 School of Criticism and Theory through a Postdoctoral Studentship awarded by its trustees. It is certainly to be hoped that similar opportunities for young faculty will continue to be available despite the general loss in recent years of public faith in the value of higher education in the humanities.

Finally, it falls to me to acknowledge that parts of this work have appeared in rather different versions in journal articles over the years. The discussion of Shelley's style in "Adonais" that appears here in chapters 2 and 4 originally formed the core of an article in *PTL*. The discussion of Wordsworth's *The Ruined Cottage,* now in chapter 3, and a number of the theoretical passages central to my model for research in poetic syntax appeared first in two separate papers published in *Language and Style*. I am extremely grateful to the editors of these journals both for their helpful comments on the prepublication texts and for their permission to rework the material here.

Despite all these kindnesses, this work could still not have seen the light of day without the assistance of Loyola's Media Services team, who beautified the figures, and of Catherine Jarrott, who held my hand during proofreading and indexing. What errors remain, I shall be happy to own.

Language

Crafted

A Theory of
Poetic Syntax

The methodological hopes of stylistics are battered
from the philosophical as well as the linguistic side.
—E. D. Hirsch, *The Aims of Interpretation.*

I

*Contemporary theories about the nature of human language
should both influence and be influenced by the analysis of literary
texts. In particular, our closest approximation to an adequate account
of the syntax of simple everyday utterances should be employed in
a mutually beneficial study of the syntax of literature.* This simple
creed lies at the heart of the discipline widely referred to today as
stylistics. This fundamental hypothesis comprises two tenets—first, a
general claim about language theory and the study of literature, and
second, a narrower application of that claim to poetic syntax. The
overall thrust of the more general statement will appear familiar to
those versed in the pertinent literature. As early as 1960, Roman
Jakobson was claiming perhaps with undue rhetorical flourish:

> [A] linguist deaf to the poetic function of language and a literary scholar
> indifferent to linguistic problems and unconversant with linguistic
> methods are equally flagrant anachronisms.[1]

The apparent inevitability of Jakobson's assertion was reemphasized
a few years later by M. A. K. Halliday in an only slightly more cau-
tious form:

> Linguistics is not and will never be the whole of literary analysis, . . .
> [but] if a text is to be described at all, then it should be described

1

properly; and this means by the theories and methods developed in linguistics.[2]

Subsequent developments have in many respects justified the confidence that both men showed. Linguistics *in its broadest sense* has performed a vital function in literary studies (equally liberally defined). Linguists' contributions to metrical theory, to cite one obvious example, have altogether transformed that particular field of inquiry.

For a while, it looked as though stylists' more specific assertion that *syntactic* analysis as such should form a vital part of critical studies might pass equally smoothly into orthodoxy. A number of excellent studies appeared which seemed to bear out Jakobson's and Halliday's optimistic forecasts even in this narrowed application. Seymour Chatman relied on a transformational analysis of present and past participial constructions in English to illustrate an important aspect of "Milton's argumentative design" in *Paradise Lost,* supporting forcefully the critical position that

> God is the implicit agent of many of those participial actions and effects. It is not necessary to mention His name; He is there by grammatical *fiat.*[3]

Donald C. Freeman examined Dylan Thomas' "A Refusal to Mourn the Death, by Fire, of a Child in London." He argued that a crucial combination of two syntactic decisions on Thomas' part (one being his decision to prepose certain syntactic material, the other being the partially entailed need to invert the subject and the auxiliary verb of the poem's opening clause) makes our experience in reading this poem one of "tension and release" particularly appropriate to an elegy.[4] We shall have occasion later in this study to discuss in detail these papers and others that have been written on similar topics. The surprising thing about their influence is that while their individual success has often been considerable, the overall critical climate has grown more, not less, hostile to stylistic analysis of this narrowly syntactic kind.

We should not look exclusively to the discipline of stylistics itself, however, if we wish to understand this development. In its early years, stylistics found itself engaged in dialog with a literary establishment most of whom still adhered to the popular doctrines of the New

Critical school. Members of the two camps might debate vigorously such issues as the separability of form from content, but they still agreed on the major goals and assumptions that critical theory should embrace. The very foundations of this gentlemanly exchange of views were rocked in the early 1970s, however, by a group of philosophically sophisticated scholars who began to dispute the validity—the very existence indeed—of major traditional literary concepts such as *text, influence, genre,* and even *author.* In the course of their argument, these theorists brought into question both the assumptions that stylists were making explicitly about the nature of the texts they examined and those that they were importing tacitly from the discipline of linguistic science.

The most famous figure in this group, Jacques Derrida, announces his general program in the following terms:

> I shall try to demonstrate why a context is never absolutely determinable, or rather, why its determination can never be entirely certain or saturated.[5]

In this and other works, Derrida asserts that the written and even the spoken word is cut adrift, severed absolutely from any well-defined source (author) or particular representation (text). That language *can* communicate meanings in the absence of both the speaker and the hearer/reader involved in the "original" context of the utterance (a context whose privilege or priority he would in any case deny) implies for Derrida that such isolation and instability are inherent in the medium:

> [A] possibility—a possible risk—is *always* possible, and is in some sense a necessary possibility.[6]

Thus Derridean criticism typically encompasses texts widely divergent in time, genre, and style, sublimating traditional judgments in these areas to the goal of broader, synthesizing interpretive insights. Furthermore, since the critic's own statements, like those of the authors he studies, are themselves autonomous and subject to interpretation, so-called deconstructionists deny even criticism an independent identity as a genre.

Derrida's position is of course not without its detractors from among the ranks of his fellow critical theorists. For a strong defense of more orthodox critical beliefs we may turn to such figures as

E. D. Hirsch. For Hirsch, the admittedly relative assurance of quasi-mathematical probability outweighs Derrida's ever-present "possible risk." Hirsch acknowledges that ultimately nothing is certain, "since the wit of man is always devising new guesses, and his curiosity is always discovering new relevant information,"[7] but he views such uncertainty as finally unimportant to the task of the literary critic:

> It is a logical mistake to confuse the impossibility of certainty in understanding with the impossibility of understanding.[8]

> Validation [of a given interpretive hypothesis] has the . . . goal of showing . . . that its likelihood of being correct is greater than or equal to that of any other known hypothesis about the text.[9]

Thus Hirsch maintains that if we are willing to suspend temporarily our awareness that all knowledge is indeed unprovable in an absolute sense, we may yet agree on a wide variety of "best-guess" approximations as strong working hypotheses. Indeed he goes further to suggest that, the laws of probability being what they are, one or more of our hypotheses may even correspond exactly with "the truth":

> Correctness is precisely the goal of interpretation and may in fact be achieved, even though it can never be known to be achieved.[10]

Contemporary critical theory, then, finds itself mired in a highly abstract debate over the nature of certainty and its relevance to critical pursuits.[11] Contributions are as likely to appear in philosophical journals as in literary periodicals, and a measure of invective is not uncommon. Hirsch's vigorous refutation of what he calls "psychologistic" theories of criticism such as that proposed by Derrida is met in turn by that author's own slashing indictment of anyone who, in the face of the evidence, remains "serenely dogmatic in regard to the intention and the origin of an utterance."[12] Without doubt, the two sides in this dispute are far from reaching a resolution.

That stylistic theory should have found itself aligned with the advocates of determinability in textual interpretation was inevitable. The whole enterprise of modern linguistic science, together with its many interdisciplinary applications, is, after all, in serious trouble if the suspicions of the Derrideans turn out to be justified.[13] To be sure, Noam Chomsky stressed from the very beginning of his work the belief that progress in linguistics, as in other scientific fields, would result from constant reevaluations of an evolving theoretical model:

> [N]either the general theory [of language structure] nor . . . particular grammars are fixed for all time. . . . Progress and revision may come from the discovery of new facts about particular languages, or from purely theoretical insights about organization of linguistic data.[14]

This doctrine, however, does not correspond to the kind of radical undecidability argued for by Derrida. Both the "general theory" and the "particular grammars" proposed at any given moment by the theoretical linguist crucially represent a Hirschean best-guess approximation (validated by means of an "objective, non-intuitive" evaluation procedure[15]) to the "system of rules" which Chomsky believes does in actual fact govern our language by "relat[ing] sound and meaning."[16] Such a view of the linguist's craft necessarily presupposes the discoverability of stable meanings in general and stylists have transferred this assumption into their own frame of reference, advocating finite, essentially discrete and accessible—though not necessarily unitary—meanings for each literary text.

The emergence and quick popularity of deconstructive criticism thus played a vitally important role in the uneven early development of stylistic theory. Most stylists, unversed in the largely philosophical tradition from which Derrida was arguing, mistook the scope of that debate and saw deconstruction as an attack on their particular analyses of specific works. In this study, by contrast, I shall largely disregard this broader issue, since I view it as altogether too radical a " 'strong' disagreement" to be dissolved using my own theory-building methods.[17] I hope only that the refinements that I propose to introduce into the fabric of stylistic theory itself will make it simpler to locate, if not to bridge, the philosophical chasm that separates all advocates of determinacy in interpretation from those who would deny its attainability.

A second kind of attack on the foundations of the discipline of stylistics has caused its practitioners altogether more proper concern. For this criticism comes, as it were, from within, from colleagues trained and adept in relating linguistic to literary analyses. Such a man is Stanley Fish. Unlike Derrida, Fish had no metaphysical difficulty early in his career in accepting the existence of a determinate text and author. Although all discourse, he maintained, was ultimately "fictional" in the sense intended by Frank Kermode,[18] Fish sided with Hirsch in the view that

> Some stories [fictions] . . . are more prestigious than others; and one story is always the standard one, the one that presents itself as uniquely true and is, in general, so accepted. . . . "Shared pretense" is what enables us to talk about anything at all.[19]

Fish's original concern, a methodological one, involved instead the process by which stylists had in the past tended to arrive at the "accepted" interpretation for which they wanted to argue and the almost absolute authority with which they then claimed to have invested it. In particular, Fish noted that stylistic theory had tended too often to omit from its picture of the interpretive process an all-important third party—the reader—while concentrating on the author and his text. The result, Fish suggested most convincingly, was an oversimplified view of the stylistic enterprise in which one read "directly from the description of a text . . . to the shape or quality of its author's mind."[20] Fish's true targets here were some early works in stylistics, such as Richard Ohmann's *Shaw: The Style and the Man* and Chatman's *The Later Style of Henry James.*[21] Fish's criticism was well taken, and his own analyses of various poetic texts demonstrated strikingly the richness that might be added to a stylistic analysis when reader-oriented factors, such as the temporal aspect of the reading process itself, were taken into account.

The discipline of stylistics reacted quickly to Fish's challenges in this area, exercising new caution in its claims and conceding certain limitations to its methodology. Although some of Fish's most sympathetic colleagues, such as Barbara Herrnstein Smith, remain unconvinced, I believe that, largely as a result of Fish's early work, most stylists today subscribe to a theory of the relationship between linguistic analysis and literary interpretation far more broad-based and far less rigid than that commonly accepted a decade ago.[22]

Fish's fine tuning of *technique* in stylistics led him however into increasingly troubled *theoretical* waters. One sees the beginnings of initially unsuspected complexity in his choice of phrasing as he restates his basically unexceptionable point about readers' individual contributions to the process of interpretation:

> [E]vidence brought to bear in the course of formalist analyses—that is, analyses generated by the assumption that meaning is embedded in the

artifact—will always point in as many directions as there are interpret-ers.[23]

In its immediate context, this sentence forms part of a determined attempt by Fish to persuade the stylist to avoid the single-minded pursuit of a unified interpretation where ambiguity or ambivalence may instead represent the most attractive reading of a passage. More broadly, though, Fish is wrestling here with the theoretical problem that consistently haunts his later work, the issue of defining *the* "the reader" whom he wishes to introduce onto the stylistic scene.

If each reader's own input vitally affects interpretive decisions, after all, and if textual evidence alone will support all readings of a text equally satisfactorily, is that not equivalent for all *practical* pur-poses to claiming with Derrida that there exists no single determin-able interpretation? Fish flirts with such a deduction:

> The large conclusion that follows . . . is that the notions of the "same" or "different" texts are fictions.[24]

And in that case, is not an honest literary critic forced to concede that he is himself "the reader," critical analysis offering, at its best, only the curiosity value inherent in one particularly skilled individual's perspective on a text that will always be unique for each reader?

Fish's own most effective work as a practical critic causes prob-lems for such a theory, as he himself is well aware. Later in his book, Fish analyzes several important interpretive cruxes in poems such as Milton's sonnet "When I consider. . . ." He astutely describes the potential conflict caused for the reader by a finite set of equally plausible interpretive responses to these passages, a stylistic feature that he identifies as the source of a certain "uneasiness" which those texts have always "inspired."[25] One cannot quarrel with these superb stylistic analyses. Yet Fish's conclusions clearly embarrass him. For if indeed textual "evidence . . . will always point in as many directions as there are interpreters," what can possibly explain that parallelism of (admittedly ambivalent) response which provides the starting point for his textual work and induces us so solidly to approve his application of the stylistic method?

To summarize: Fish's objections to what he sees as an awkwardly mechanistic school of stylistics find their solution in his championing of the reader; the need to allow for the reader's contribution to the interpretive process will guarantee that stylistic analyses take on greater flexibility, flexibility which *in theory* appears limitless and even uncontrollable; yet *in practice* even Fish's own textual readings assume a level of consensus that belies this alleged randomness of response. Fish's means of escape from the contradiction between his theory and his practice is to propose the "interpretive community," a socioculturally determined grouping of individuals who "share interpretive strategies" and thus experience a given text in broadly similar ways:

> What I have been arguing is that meanings come already calculated . . . because language is always perceived . . . within a structure of norms. That structure, however, is not abstract and independent but social, . . . a structure that changes when one situation, with its assumed background of practices, purposes, and goals, has given way to another.[26]

Only such an approach will allow Fish the luxury of continuing to practice critical analysis while appearing to maintain his close link with the "real" world of the actual, individual reader or with *"meaning as an event,"* as he terms it.[27]

By the end of *Is There a Text in This Class?* then, Fish has painted himself into a corner. He has rejected, as "abstract and independent" grounds for supporting a critical interpretation, the kind of syntactic analysis typical of modern linguistics. Yet his interpretive communities do little more than paper over the cracks left by this major structural work, evolving finally into an elaborate procedural excuse for conducting critical business as usual:

> [O]ne wonders what implications it [Fish's argument for interpretive communities] has for the practice of literary criticism. The answer is, none whatsoever.[28]

It is thus disturbing to discover that Fish's implicit challenge to stylistics in this broad theoretical area has in general been less well answered than his more narrowly methodological points. This is not, I think, because his arguments are faultless. Rather, it is because the convinced stylist's response on this broad front, if it is to win general approval, must originate in a comprehensive theory of stylistic analysis, a theory whose aims and claims are as clearly articulated as its methods and terms. And it is in precisely this area that stylistics as a critical school remains most sadly deficient, lacking any sustained theoretical account of the discipline *as a whole.*

On the one hand, the specifically stylistic literature has consisted largely of essay anthologies.[29] Inevitably, contributors to these volumes have found themselves unable to spare the space to set their particular discoveries within a complete theoretical framework. On the other hand, while a number of book-length theoretical studies *have* addressed in greater depth the application to literature of concepts from linguistic theory, these works have focused for the most part on areas neighboring, but not central to, the study of simple syntactic analysis—areas such as literary history, metrics, the theory of language processing, and speech-act theory.[30] In the field of literary syntax, narrowly interpreted, no such comprehensive theoretical overview has been attempted.

I find no great difficulty in identifying the standards that we should expect such a theoretical overview to meet.

(a) It should delimit clearly the range of phenomena for which an account is to be proposed. This preliminary step reduces the danger of subsequent misunderstandings about the adequacy of the account itself.

(b) It should offer a well-articulated, fully defined theoretical model, probably consisting of two components: a set of theoretical constructs or categories and a description of the way(s) in which those constructs or categories relate to one another.

(c) It should evaluate the capacity of the proposed model to analyze appropriate data in an elegant and insightful way. This will generally involve detailed application of the model to specific textual examples.

(d) And, finally, it should examine the implications of its conclusions for associated fields, anticipating objections wherever possible and illustrating potential practical applications.

In what remains of this chapter, I shall outline a linguistic theory of poetic syntax which I believe meets these goals. In the chapters that follow, I shall elaborate on certain of its provisions and extend its exemplification to cover a fairly broad spectrum of authors and texts.

To the extent that I thus succeed in establishing the effectiveness of my theoretical model, this study will by all means represent an indirect response to the skepticism about stylistics expressed by Fish, Smith, and others. At the same time I shall rely heavily on their cautionary tales, and hope rather to overcome Fish's self-imposed obstacles and restore his faith in his own stylistic skills than altogether to demolish his position. Since I have already noted my unwillingness to take on at all the disciples of deconstruction, the task that I have set myself may be viewed as that of restoring the damaged fabric of what I take to be stylistics' basically sound but dilapidated structure, a task we may best begin by examining its foundations.

II

It is the stylist's contention that one major force working to ensure a measure of conformity in readers' reactions to literary texts is their substantial shared inventory of techniques for analyzing the linguistic behavior taking place around them. Of course, any individual's response to a given text will depend to some extent on features entirely idiosyncratic to him—limitations on his attention span, deficiencies in his vocabulary, his unfamiliarity with a particular typeface. To some extent, too, that response will be attributable to extrasyntactic conventions governing language use of the kind well discussed in works such as Smith's *On the Margins of Discourse* or Mary Louise Pratt's *Toward a Speech Act Theory of Discourse*. Nor, finally, would I want to rule out of the total, overall picture factors unique to the *process* of reading itself, those " 'computational systems' whereby hearers and readers interpret sentences."[31] But we may safely leave discussion of these influences on interpretation to one side as we pursue our specifically stylistic theory. Their parallel importance qualifies and contextualizes, but cannot negate, the "fundamental condition" governing our perception of any "propositional structure," the condition that that perception "must . . . be based on a grammatical analysis of the sentence."[32] By holding these ancillary considerations in abeyance, in fact, we shall simply be focusing our attention more clearly on that broad area of agreement about what the language of a given text involves that modern linguistic science refers to as native speakers' common linguistic "competence."[33] In certain instances, the shared techniques that we all bring into play as a part of this competence may be broadly cognitive, applying to linguistic phenomena as a "special case."[34] In others they may apply uniquely in our processing of specifically linguistic information. Whatever the nature of such subdivisions, however, the mere existence of this rather broad-based unanimity about language, its structure, and its meaning, is as fundamental to stylistics as it is to linguistic theory.[35] As its presence accounts in part for the ease and apparent success with which we communicate at all from day to day, so too it can form the basis for our understanding of what the language of a literary work offers to its readers.

If, then, we rely on this liberal definition of linguistic competence, we may safely view the function of stylistic analysis as being that of explicating the relationship between readers' shared syntactic competence and their similarly shared "experience" of a given text. The assumption that human linguistic communication works through a set of rule-governed processes relating sound to meaning —which include syntactic processes, among others—itself guarantees that at least some aspects of the literary experience of that text *will* be shared by all its readers. The stylist merely seeks to discover the means by which language's role in shaping that experience is exercised.

In a particular case, the stylist may of course choose to limit himself to some specialized syntactic "subcompetence" when developing his analysis. Examining a text from some literary period other than his own, for example, he may opt either to analyze the part played by syntactic conventions of his own time in establishing the text's interpretation, or to undertake the linguistic research necessary to approach that text in terms of the syntactic system of the period in which it was written. (Indeed, one or the other choice is presumably unavoidable wherever those historical periods are widely separated.) Many stylists will similarly restrict the breadth of the interpretive issues they address. Fish isolates a fairly small number of textually problematic passages in his essay "Interpreting the *Variorum*" and asks very specific questions about which of several editorial decisions would be preferred in each instance on the basis of evidence from syntactic analysis of the text.[36] Yet no such narrowed focus, either linguistic or interpretive, is absolutely required. Indeed, the unmarked case for stylistic analysis might be argued to be precisely that in which the terms "syntactic competence" and "interpretation of the text" are given their broadest, most intuitive scope.

It may seem that I have now merely redefined Fish's interpretive communities as groups of native speakers sharing a given linguistic competence (or subcompetence). To the extent that this is so, I consider it an appropriate reformulation. But Fish himself could by no means go along with my revision. As his remark cited above about "shared pretense" as the basis for rational discourse clearly shows, Fish is certainly aware that stylistic criticism must indulge in a measure of abstraction and idealization. But what distinguishes our positions is precisely Fish's unwillingness to take the further step of attributing any part of individual readers' shared response to a work of literature directly to those readers' *linguistic* relatedness, to their common knowledge of a given language. He believes instead that

> I can speak and presume to be understood by someone . . . *not . . . because he and I share a language,* in the sense of knowing the meanings of individual words and the rules for combining them, but because a way of thinking . . . shares us, and implicates us in a world of already-in-place objects, purposes, goals, procedures, values, and so on.[37]

It should by all means be stressed at this point that I have no wish to deny the importance of many altogether nonlinguistic factors that undoubtedly do enhance the cohesiveness of groups of readers already bound closely together by their linguistic knowledge—factors such as their perceptions of genre or of literary period. My argument is merely that we should bypass such matters in stylistic theory, leaving them as raw material for a separate though allied discipline, the description of "literary competence" in the sense intended by Jonathan Culler in his *Structuralist Poetics*. I side with Culler, that is, in ceding this admittedly fertile territory to a discipline that begins where stylistic analysis leaves off, a field whose mandate is to explain how "the 'grammar' of literature" leads readers "to convert linguistic sequences into literary structures and meanings."[38] While the importance of accepted literary categories and the evolution of certain analytical procedures within a given social group are certainly fascinating topics for discussion, their inclusion in the field of stylistic studies only muddies already clouded waters. Worst of all, it obscures the one crucial and isolable feature that does bind together all readers of a given text—its language—and thus hamstrings the stylist, requiring him constantly to work through or around material outside his area of expertise.

My restricting the goals of stylistics to the discovery of relationships between syntactic competence and shared interpretive experience will be criticized by those who accept a view broadly similar to
Fish's in that those relationships emerge only by virtue of a further
idealization, an additional layer of abstraction (away from the experience of the actual reader in his fireside chair) superimposed on my
prior insistence that syntactic competence itself be viewed as a theoretical abstraction.[39] If I concede this charge, however, I by no means
surrender the field, for I refuse to see abstraction as necessarily or
universally evil. As I shall show in detail in the coming chapters, just
as with any other pre-theoretical assumption, the "cost" of hypothe-
sizing both a shared syntactic competence and a shared literary experience should be assessed *a posteriori* in light of the insights and
clarifications that it permits. Since my aim is to develop a method of
literary criticism based on linguistic principles yet reaching out beyond linguistic analysis to make broader, literarily challenging
claims, the final justification for proposing a certain kind of "reader,"
not necessarily identical with any specific reader in the real world,
will be the attractiveness of the critical ends that that proposal pro-
motes. Fish's reservations about stylistics derive their force from the
altogether different assumption that stylistic analyses may be justified by what might be called a "naive linguistic realism." We shall
have to return to this issue in far greater detail toward the very end
of this study.

   Our next task, then, is to develop a theoretical model capable of
effectively and elegantly characterizing the complex relationship
between syntactic competence and literary interpretation. Stylistics,
I shall suggest in what follows, involves the analyst in three qualita-
tively distinct activities.

(a) In the *technical* phase of his study, the stylist formally captures
    purely syntactic processes that contribute to a given text's lin-
    guistic identity. His judgments in this area derive (ideally in a
    tightly constrained manner) from similarly technical statements
    made about the standard language in syntactic theory. In partic-
    ular, the stylist borrows both his methodological principles and
    his terminology in this phase of his work directly from linguistic
    science, and his commentary on a text thus parallels in literary
    studies the work of the dialectologist or the sociolinguist in

analyzing geographically and socially specialized languages respectively.

(b) A second facet of the stylist's work involves examining the interaction between the syntactic features of a text and certain independent aesthetic forms. If he characterizes some syntactic structure as "symmetrical," after all, the stylist has stepped beyond the bounds of simple linguistic theory, which recognizes no such concept as symmetry in its inventory. Similarly, although "movement" may be defined linguistically, the associated notion of "distance" is not generally so specified. Their importance to stylistic theory demands that we develop a separate classification for concepts of this sort; I shall employ the term *perceptual* to refer to this category of stylistic statements.

(c) Finally (and most controversially), the stylist operates at an *interpretive* level to correlate both technical and perceptual observations about some text with his own or others' essentially independent interpretations of its content. I use the term "correlate" here deliberately, since, as I shall reemphasize in chapter 4, even at the interpretive level the stylist does not employ linguistic analysis to "uncover" some previously unsuspected, but now magically indisputable, meaning. At best, stylistic evidence may combine with data from other sources—biographical, historical, metrical, or "new critical"—to elucidate problem areas, isolate poetic cruxes, and suggest solutions to critical impasses.

A couple of remarks about this preliminary formulation are in order. I have used three different terms to describe the three components that constitute my model for a theory of poetic syntax: "(technical) *phase*," "(perceptual) *facet*," and "(interpretive) *level*." Each represents a different metaphorical view of the stylistic endeavor. Of the three, the first and last attract me simply as expository conveniences because both appear routinely in prepositional phrases ("in the . . . phase" and "at the . . . level"); I can find no equivalent prepositional frame for "facet." But the temporal metaphor ("phase") is too easily confused with nonmetaphorical descriptions of the actual reading process—a confusion I am particularly anxious to avoid. (At no stage should my theory be viewed as an exact description of *how we read* poetry, a point I again return to in chapter 5.) I am thus forced back upon the term "level," whose spatial content may imply a hierarchical relationship with which I am also distinctly uncomfortable. Where the word occurs, therefore, it should always be taken to allude simply to one aspect of the stylistic relationship whose richly multi-"faceted" nature we are trying to describe.

Nor do I seek to suggest through my preliminary formulation of this model that every stylistic analysis necessarily contains (or should contain) comments at all three theoretical levels. E. R. Steinberg justly contends that a formal linguistic analysis may provide important insights into the style of a literary text even when its author makes no attempt to indicate any aesthetic or interpretive functions associated with the technical features he isolates.[40] One can perhaps less easily imagine a stylistic account that succeeded in drawing valid interpretive conclusions while omitting pertinent technical and perceptual observations; indeed, the belief in such a possibility too often tempts the critic to develop interpretations on the basis of presumed syntactic facts that later turn out not to fit the mold designed for them. Elsewhere, however, I have demonstrated that a situation may indeed arise in which technical statements demand only minimal attention during the development of a stylistically sophisticated argument, interpretive conclusions thus completely dominating the analysis.[41] In summary, the *worth* of a stylistic argument should by no means be assessed on the basis simply of the number of theoretical levels to which it may succeed in referring.

The next three chapters of this study develop, respectively, my accounts of the technical, perceptual, and interpretive levels of a stylistic theory of poetic syntax. In chapter 2, I concentrate on methodological questions, comparing and evaluating the techniques that stylists use first to develop and then to substantiate their formal descriptions of the language of a text. In chapter 3, the emphasis falls on extending in various directions the taxonomy of commonly accepted perceptual effects, while chapter 4 focuses for the most part on what I maintain has been a major omission from the literature in the field until now—the analysis of rhetorical, nonmimetic poetic syntax. As this brief preview suggests, the topics demanding most careful treatment differ widely as we move from level to level within the theory. My discussion will also inevitably sidestep altogether a variety of important and interesting questions in each area, though

I do hope to provide sufficient material in the notes to each chapter to ensure that even these matters can be pursued by the reader who is interested in a more comprehensive picture.

To the same general end, I also include in each chapter a large number of practical examples of stylistic analysis, in the hope that the reader will be able to construct from them a clearer understanding of the stylistic approach that I advocate as it would work in practice. The examples that I have chosen may strike the reader as somewhat limited in scope; for the most part, they are taken from those areas in which I myself have read most thoroughly—English literature of the seventeenth, eighteenth, and nineteenth centuries. While I freely acknowledge this bias, I would contend that it in no way detracts from the validity or the usefulness of my conclusions. A theory need not be exhaustive to be comprehensive; where particular stylistic possibilities go unnoticed, the theory should still, if correctly formulated, be able to encompass and integrate them as soon as their importance has been proved.

Before moving ahead, I should finally note that I shall not elsewhere justify the arbitrary limitation of my study to the syntax of *poetic* texts. This limitation results in part from sheer historical accident (my interest in stylistics having grown out of, and remained closely allied with, my love of English Romantic poetry). But in part, too, it is due to my recognition that to encompass the analysis of prose style would demand a major new allocation of time and space. It may indeed prove possible to apply the techniques and categories described here directly to prose analysis. I tend to side with Pratt in seeing this commensurability between the stylistic analysis of prose and poetry as a desirable outcome in principle.[42] Whether it will indeed turn out to be the case, however, remains an empirical issue which I do not want to prejudge without substantially greater research.[43]

The Technical Analysis of a Literary Text

Criticism in English ought to have a hunger for a
sound linguistics.
                                    —Harold Whitehall,
                                "From Linguistics to Criticism"

I

Robert Frost's famous comment that "writing free verse is like playing tennis with the net down" makes a big rhetorical splash but badly misstates the logic of free verse composition. It makes no allowance for the poet's ability to fashion his own challenging and effective rules for the creative "game." The analogy functions far better if we employ it instead to combat the dangerous misconception that one might reasonably undertake a *technical stylistic analysis* without determining in advance the constraints proper to that particular activity. In a pursuit whose goal is, I have argued, an accurate as well as formally efficient description of a text's language, the rules are "constitutive"; they do not "regulate" the discipline, to paraphrase Jonathan Culler, "so much as create the possibility" of its succeeding at all.[1] Altering or overriding the rules by brute force, therefore, could easily transform what began as a tennis match into a joust or even a purposeless melee.

In view of this danger, it is surprising to find that few books and articles in the recent literature offer clear methodological guidelines to the aspiring analyst. Many stylists merely assert, rather than demonstrate, the relevance of transformational or structuralist grammars, case grammar, or speech-act theory, to their particular texts. Where the language of those texts happens to include syntactically marginal or nonstandard forms, furthermore, they readily take a wide variety of theoretically extreme steps in their efforts to account for the perceived deviance.

Stylists who have shown any interest in justifying their analytical methods have usually claimed that their interpretive ends excused whatever extraordinary technical means they invoked. Too superficial a reading of such literary critics as John Reichert may appear at first to lend this laid-back approach a certain air of respectability. Reichert suggests that pragmatic justification must ultimately figure in our evaluation of any critical argument:

> To regard criticism as aiming not just at true statements about, but at new perceptions of a literary work, is to admit among the others a purely pragmatic test for its success. . . . That is, one test of an interpretation is whether it actually provides the reader with the new way of perceiving that it is intended to provide him with.[2]

As will become clear in chapter 4, I have a great deal of sympathy for Reichert's position when it comes to considering the critical (that is the technical or perceptual *and* the interpretive) act as a whole. But we must take great care not to confuse the task of interpreting a text with that of analyzing its linguistic form.[3] Reichert's suggestion that we aim *"not just* at true statements" about a text implies that truth as such does indeed have a place in literary studies; that place would seem to me to be, if anywhere, at the technical level of stylistic analysis. Here, objectivity and accuracy are at a premium, the careful formulation of adequate methodological "means" thus demanding the most careful attention.

I will not belabor this point, since Mary Louise Pratt has already argued it with great vigor. Employing an analogy from the work-bench rather than the tennis court, she insists that the right to apply in stylistic research the methods of formal syntax brings with it attendant responsibilities. All too often, she complains,

> the poetician is left with no theoretical obligations to linguistics. He is set free to raid the linguist's toolbox at will and to use what he finds in whatever way he likes.[4]

In this chapter, then, I shall take as read Pratt's arguments and those of others who have asserted the stylist's "theoretical obligations to linguistics," focusing instead on the logically subsequent task of defining those obligations as precisely as possible. I shall take as my point of departure a review of some specific practical problems that arise if one adopts a recklessly laissez-faire attitude toward the technical side of stylistics. My solutions to those problems will in turn motivate certain more general "rules of thumb" concerning proper and improper ways of developing stylistic analyses. Finally, I shall particularly emphasize the need for the stylist to develop a controlled sequence of analytical steps by which he will proceed in order to ensure the richest possible technical account of each text he examines.

II

The stylist's first obligation as an analyst of technique is to make every possible effort to account for the syntactic form of his text as a *sample of,* rather than as an *exception to,* the language in which it was written. Such a description of our goal should not be taken to imply that stylistics never involves itself with devising nonstandard grammars; I shall turn to that topic in due course. It does entail that every effort should be made *in the first instance* to avoid such a step by analyzing a poetic text using only the methods and terms accepted by linguistic science for describing the standard language. As Pratt again points out, we should guard against any step that

> obscures the real relation that holds between poetic utterances and the grammar of the language in which they are written, ... the relation that all utterances in a given language hold with respect to the grammar.[5]

Whatever the temptation to innovate, the primacy of this fundamental relationship must be preserved.

Such a principle is fully consonant with Paul Kiparsky's observations in his eminently reasonable essay "The Role of Linguistics in a Theory of Poetry." From his study of linguistic behavior in languages around the globe that is considered "poetic," Kiparsky concludes that *"the linguistic [elements] which are potentially relevant in poetry are just those which are potentially relevant in grammar."*[6] All that I now propose is the correlative procedural guideline: stylists should curb their more creative linguistic urges so that the analyses they propose will in fact fall within the scope of Kiparsky's observational generalization. Indeed, I would further endorse the slightly narrower prescription that stylistic analysis initially employ not only linguistically salient "building blocks" (the metaphor is Kiparsky's) but also the protocols and patterns for combining those blocks dictated by everyday usage. Where Kiparsky, then, detects "homologies" between standard and poetic syntax,[7] I would mandate identity, at least where the literary data are compatible with such an approach.

The necessity for so strong a procedural requirement must, of course, be established on purely theoretical grounds by producing evidence that a failure to respect its provisions may result in major critical oversights. At the same time, we may note in passing that it corresponds to a highly common-sense view of the reader's strategy as he approaches a text. Equipped virtually since birth with an acute facility for processing the language around him, why would the reader choose to reject that facility in reading poetry unless some aspect of its linguistic form actively forced him to do so? Put this way, the moral seems self-evident; yet as a methodological principle it is easily lost to view.

An important decision facing even the stylist who accepts my first point about technical analysis involves the choice of a *specific* syntactic theory within which to proceed. I remarked earlier that all empirical hypotheses, including hypotheses about human language, are vulnerable to scientific progress and destined for obsolescence in the long run.[8] I noted too, however, that in the short run they still represent conscientious attempts to explain "the truth" about the phenomena they describe. A discredited theory is thus in an important sense "wrong" and the stylist has an obligation to rely for his technical material only on those theories of language that have not been disproved. I find it hard, for instance, to imagine a strong stylistic argument based on the once-important contrast in American structuralist linguistics between "exocentric" and "endocentric" constructions, at least as it was originally formulated by linguists such as Leonard Bloomfield.[9] Advances in linguistic theory have made it difficult to accept as fundamental a binary categorization of syntactic structures that places the constructions *in the house* and *if John ran away* in one category, *boys and girls* and *very fresh milk* in the second. If he seeks an accurate and revealing account of the language of his poetic text, the stylist will certainly need to avoid such obvious anachronisms and work only with the most recent analytical tools.

For the present, I would contend, transformational generative

grammars still offer the most widely accessible, linguistically re-
spectable account of syntactic structure and syntactic processes.
Most useful of these grammars, furthermore, is that version of
transformational syntactic theory developed in papers and books by
linguists such as Joan Bresnan, Noam Chomsky, Joseph Emonds,
Ray Jackendoff, and John R. Ross.[10] This is not to pretend that the
set of assumptions from which all these authors may be said to have
taken their lead and to which each has in turn contributed—the
so-called Extended Standard Theory—has been without its critics.
As Bresnan rightly points out in discussing "the familiar *Aspects*
model," "subsequent research has shown that each of [the] properties of the model is incorrect," and, inevitably, competing theories
—"Montague Grammar"; Gazdar, Pullum, and Sag's "Generalized
Phrase-Structure Grammar"; and Bresnan and Kaplan's own "Lexi-
cal-Functional Grammar"—have arisen in response to these perceived inadequacies.[11] Nor, of course, can the theoretical linguist
afford to undervalue even the most limited of these divergencies
between theories:

> How can we choose among these various theories? From a broad philo-
> sophical perspective, it is not necessary to do so. . . . But from a scientific
> perspective . . . we must find or construct the best theory.[12]

When we as stylists seek to apply linguistic theory to poetic texts,
however, a second, more pragmatic consideration must also influence our choice. Ironically, it is again Bresnan who offers the most
realistic rationale for adhering *pro tempore* to the Extended Standard Theory (EST), even though it has come under such heavy fire:

> [T]his is still the picture that many linguists and psychologists [and
> critics] have of a transformational grammar, a fact that attests both to
> the intuitive appeal of the model and to its enormous fruitfulness in
> guiding linguistic research.[13]

As my argument in the preceding paragraphs dictates, should one or
another of the theories now in open competition with the EST finally
succeed in usurping its current position as the linguistic orthodoxy,
stylists will have to adjust to its modes of analysis and description. For
our present purposes, however, a very slightly modified version of
the EST would seem still to offer an excellent blend of the twin
virtues of easy familiarity and technical respectability.

As detailed analyses of particular passages necessitate, I shall in the course of this study elaborate on specific aspects of the EST. A broad overview at this point, however, may help to keep such observations in their proper perspective. Modern syntactic theory, then, hypothesizes several *components* to a grammar. Taken together, these components describe the numerous and complexly interlocking regularities that constitute a native speaker's syntactic competence. Every lexical item in the language, for instance, is assumed to belong to one of a small number of *lexical categories* each of which is in turn defined by the broadly similar behavior of its members in equivalent syntactic contexts. Each lexical category is assigned a *label* [Noun (or N); Verb (V); Adjective (ADJ); Adverb (ADV); Preposition (P)] and a set of *phrase-structure rules* then describes permissible combinations of these categories in the language. For them to achieve this description economically, it turns out to be necessary that the phrase-structure rules combine lexical categories into *phrasal units* [Noun Phrase (or NP); Verb Phrase (VP) etc.] before using those intermediate syntactic structures themselves to build *clausal* and *sentential* constructions (S). The phrase-structure rules thus *generate* (or define) a hierarchical structure for each sentence loosely equivalent to that assigned in some previous theories by "immediate constituent analysis."[14]

Idiosyncratic information that determines for each individual word its appropriate syntactic and semantic context is contained in that word's *subcategorization* and *selection restrictions* respectively. These formal conditions govern the insertion of lexical items into the abstract structures generated by the phrase-structure grammar *(lexical insertion),* ensuring, for example, that the verb *put* will appear only in sentences where it is followed syntactically by both a nominal object and a locative prepositional phrase ("Sherlock Holmes put *a briar pipe into his mouth*") and that the verb *enjoy* will be used only when its subject displays the semantic property of being human or at least animate.

All of the rule types described in the preceding two paragraphs combine to generate theoretical constructs called *deep* or *underlying syntactic structures.* These structures may be portrayed diagrammatically in various formally equivalent ways. Linguists often use *labeled bracketings,* as in the notation

[S[NP[N Bill]] [VP[V sat] [PP[P down]]]].

But so-called *tree-structures* are often easier to appreciate at a glance and will be widely used in this study. A deep-structure tree for the sentence *Bill sat down* might look like Figure 1.

Deep structures in turn serve as input to a set of *transformational rules* which alter them in very narrowly restricted ways to derive further *intermediate structures.* Since both deep and intermediate structures are subject to transformational alteration, a full syntactic *derivation* may consist of a string of several structures each related pairwise with either one or two other structures by specific transformational rules. Thus to derive the sentence *Down Bill sat!* we need to apply at least one transformation to a deep structure identical to that for *Bill sat down.* The *Prepositional-Phrase (PP) Fronting* rule, to be precise, will move the post-verbal PP to the beginning of the sentence, giving the surface structure in Figure 2.[15]

The syntactician manipulates lexical, phrase-structure, and transformational components of the grammar to devise an overall system that is elegant in that it accurately and with maximum economy reflects relevant generalizations about the language's structure. In many cases, this may involve positing deep or even intermediate structures that are noticeably "abstract," far divorced from what we would immediately recognize as an English sentence. The permissi-

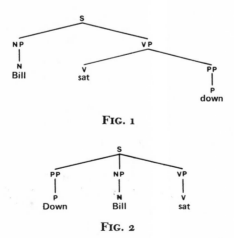

FIG. 1

FIG. 2

bility of such abstraction, when linked with a number of other formal considerations, makes transformational grammars extremely powerful tools. Transformational syntacticians realized early in the evolution of this theory, therefore, that restrictions would need to be placed on the operation of transformations if they were not to "overgenerate" wildly, producing not only structures commonly attested in the language, but also a wide variety of highly counterintuitive constructions. First came the imposition of a specific *ordering* on transformational rules; it was shown that, unless applied in this invariant order, transformations would predict hopelessly unacceptable sentences. Next linguists discovered that, in deriving sentences that contained more than one clause, it was necessary not only to apply the rules in that same order, but also to repeat the full *cycle* of rules for each clause separately (beginning with the clause most deeply *embedded*).

Even this additional restriction, however, did not account for a wide variety of cases in which sentences predicted to be grammatical by the transformational component failed to satisfy common-sense criteria for acceptability. A set of *constraints* and *conditions* on transformations was therefore proposed in the late 1960s, the investigation of which quickly became, and has since remained, a major focus of syntactic research. These constraints and conditions formalize restrictions that the language imposes on *all* of its major transformational operations, and may be written so as to affect either the formal statement of the transformational rules themselves or their mode of application to particular kinds of syntactic structures.[16] Some even define the acceptability of a given surface structure *after* it has been through the transformational cycle.[17]

The transformational syntactician's ultimate goal in all of these theoretical additions and revisions has been to devise a set of rules, suitably constrained, that will apply to deep structures to derive a set of *surface structures* corresponding exactly to "all and only" the acceptable sentences of the language under study.

As may be clear from this summary, transformational grammar possesses enormous explanatory power, power whose existence worries the linguist, whose constant attention has been devoted to taming it.[18] It offers a correspondingly strong temptation to his colleague in stylistics who is often unaware of the theoretical monster he is capable of fashioning. With its aid he can easily describe a wide variety of syntactic structures—real or imagined, thinkable or absurd, "poetic" or "prosaic." Indeed, were he really free to "raid the linguist's toolbox" as Pratt fears, the stylist could devise a hundred different ways to account for any given line of his text. Rather than dazzling us, then, the almost boundless capacities of the linguistic model that we rely on should instead alert us to the very real dangers of deviating from the relatively safe and well-trodden ground of a specific grammar of English when beginning the stylistic analysis of a poetic text.

III

The particular kind of blind spot that may develop if the stylist pays insufficient attention to the demands of the standard grammar when developing his argument is well illustrated in the extensive literature devoted to E. E. Cummings' "anyone lived in a pretty how town."[19] (For those who may be unfamiliar with it, I have included a text of this ballad on a separate page.)

Any number of technical problems confront the stylistic analyst approaching this poem. Of these, one major concern will be the formal account to be given of Cummings' use of the word *anyone*, which occurs in lines 1, 6, 16, 25, and 31. The specific cause for this concern will be the fact that a typical syntactic account of the English language bars the word *any* and its derivative compounds such as *anyone* and *anywhere* from appearing in certain clearly defined types of sentence. As Otto Jespersen explains,

> *Any* indicates one or more, no matter which; therefore *any* is *very frequent in sentences implying negation* or doubt (questions, conditions).[20]

Indeed, *any* and its derivatives turn out to be almost invariably *unacceptable* in simple declarative sentences unless those sentences contain a negative word such as *not, noone,* or *never:*

*I went out on *any* occasion.[21]
I did *not* go out on *any* occasion.

With these examples before him, the analyst finds himself forced to rule Cummings' constructions in lines 1, 16, and 25 grammatically deviant by the standards of everyday usage:

anyone lived in a pretty how town

anyone lived in a pretty how town
(with up so floating many bells down)
spring summer autumn winter
he sang his didn't he danced his did.

Women and men (both little and small)   5
cared for anyone not at all
they sowed their isn't they reaped their same
sun moon stars rain

children guessed (but only a few
and down they forgot as up they grew   10
autumn winter spring summer)
that noone loved him more by more

when by now and tree by leaf
she laughed his joy she cried his grief
bird by snow and stir by still   15
anyone's any was all to her

someones married their everyones
laughed their cryings and did their dance
(sleep wake hope and then) they
said their nevers they slept their dream   20

stars rain sun moon
(and only the snow can begin to explain
how children are apt to forget to remember
with up so floating many bells down)

one day anyone died i guess   25
(and noone stooped to kiss his face)
busy folk buried them side by side
little by little and was by was

all by all and deep by deep
and more by more they dream their sleep   30
noone and anyone earth by april
wish by spirit and if by yes.

Women and men (both dong and ding)
summer autumn winter spring
reaped their sowing and went their came   35
sun moon stars rain

anyone lived in a pretty how town
anyone's any was all to her
one day *anyone* died

Indeed, the problem runs deeper than this, since an additional constraint on the use of *any-* in day-to-day contexts requires that the
negative word that forms so vital a part of its immediate context also
appear to the left of (that is before, not after) the word *any-* itself:

I went out on each occasion.
On each occasion I went out.

I did *not* go out on *any* occasion.
*On *any* occasion I did *not* go out.

Although, as the first pair of sentences demonstrates, PP-Fronting
can routinely prepose phrases structurally analogous to *on any occasion,* such movement is prohibited, probably by a simple filter oper-
ating at the level of surface structure, if it would result in a surface
misalignment of *any-* and its associated negative element. Yet Cummings has chosen in lines 5 and 6 to overlook or transgress this
constraint:[22]

Women and men . . .
cared for *anyone not* at all.

This choice appears all the more significant upon reflection, since a
syntactically more standard alternative involves only the most minor
adjustment to the text:

Women and men . . .
did *not* care for *anyone* at all.

The task that confronts the stylist here is one that recurs constantly in subtly different forms whenever he involves himself with
technical analysis. A formal statement needs to be made about a
construction which the standard grammar will not generate and
which we should therefore label unacceptable, deviant, or ungrammatical. In order to appreciate fully some of the many options available to the stylist under these circumstances, let us briefly examine
the work of two scholars, Samuel R. Levin and James Peter Thorne,
both of whom have mapped out plans of attack for the technical anal-

ysis of this particular poem that are *prima facie* worthy of serious consideration.[23]

Levin proposes that, in analyzing a deviant syntactic construction from a poetic text, we should begin from the rules of the standard grammar, adjusting them as little as is necessary to generate the attested material:

> [We] assume, first of all, that the grammar will not generate them. . . . We then ask how the grammatical rules can be fixed so as to generate the sentence in question.[24]

He further suggests that such adjustment can usually be accomplished "in one of two ways: a new rule may be introduced; or items may be shifted from class to class."[25] In his paper, Levin applies this method exclusively to line 4 of Cummings' poem and in particular to the phrase "he danced his did." But we can extrapolate from that discussion to determine the approach he probably would adopt to our own current problem, the appearance of *anyone* in syntactically nonstandard contexts.

One of Levin's two proposed methods of adjusting the grammar would here involve eliminating from the syntactic features accompanying the word *anyone* all hints that it differs from other indefinite pronouns such as *someone* or *everyone*. This step would effectively "shift" *anyone* as an element in the language of this particular poem from a "class" of its own into a broader class of pronouns with fewer restrictions on their syntactic placement. Alternatively, the stylist might select Levin's other option and adjust a "rule" of the standard syntax when writing a formal description of Cummings' work. In this particular case it would not be appropriate to "introduce a new rule"; instead one would simply drop from the grammar the troublesome filter that, in standard English, determines the acceptability of sentences containing *any-* on the basis of certain negative words' presence and relative position in the syntactic context. But whether we choose to adjust the class membership of *anyone* in the lexicon or to relax the constraint on its appearance in surface structure, it should be noted that the final outcome will be much the same: *anyone* will be ruled fully acceptable in this specific poetic context by virtue of Levin's tampering with ("fixing") standard syntactic conventions. It is this conclusion, with its implicit assumption that syntactic deviance should be explained away by the stylist, rather than simply observed, that seems to me a dangerous one. To be sure, Levin subsequently demands that the stylist compare the extended grammar that he has devised for some work of literature with the standard grammar to assess the effects of his adjustments. By then, however, as I shall shortly show, the damage will already have been done, since the risk of oversight exists *as soon as* the standard grammar is overridden in favor of an extraordinary syntactic analysis.

Thorne roundly rejects any approach to the technical analysis of poetic syntax which, like Levin's, takes the standard grammar as its basis. He argues that a poetic text should instead be treated as pristine linguistic data, as "a sample of a different language, or a different dialect."[26] The stylist, he contends, should devise categories and rules whose only justification is that they best characterize the language of the text currently at hand. The syntax that Thorne develops for Cummings' poem thus involves lexical categories and, by implication at least, phrase-structure rules wholly foreign to the standard language. To give just one example, Thorne's "Class A" words are characterized by three syntactic features: they appear only in object position; they are always preceded by possessive pronouns; and they never appear with adjectival modifiers. The class thus defined includes the words *did* and *didn't* from line 4, *joy* and *grief* from line 14, and *dream* from line 20. Needless to say, such a classification has no application whatsoever to standard usage. Thorne's ultimate goal is to write a syntax for this poem which both accounts for the sentences Cummings actually uses and, additionally, characterizes unattested sentences (such as *Anyone kissed his children*) which, Thorne claims, we feel instinctively to " 'belong' to the same language as that in which the poem is written."[27]

We do not need to infer Thorne's probable attitude towards our own problem with the syntactic analysis of this poem, since he discusses the question explicitly in his essay:

> Another group of words which are most conveniently treated as nouns includes *no one* [sic], *anyone, someones* and *everyones*.[28]

Thorne simply categorizes these words along with more standard nouns such as *children* (line 9) in his "Class C." In so doing, he predicts that a sentence such as *Women kissed their children* will enjoy the same degree of acceptability within the context of this poem as the sentence *Someones kissed their anyone.* Since, in fact, his method assumes *a priori* that whatever appears in the text should be defined as acceptable by the specialized grammar for which it provides the only data, the appearance of *anyone* in lines 1, 6, 16, and 25 *necessarily* receives his approval despite the distinctly odd sound that I believe those sentences would have for the naive reader. There is in fact no mechanism in Thorne's stylistic theory, no formal procedure, for recognizing ungrammaticality.

What previous approaches to the technical description of this poem have in common, then, is an incautious eagerness to discuss ways of extending (Levin) or totally recasting (Thorne) the grammar on the grounds of the deviant constructions it manifests. The authors cited here appear to have left out of consideration the possibility of analyzing the poem strictly according to the canons of the standard language. Significantly, both Levin and Thorne would, I suspect, miss what I take to be a crucial observation about the role of the word *anyone* in "anyone lived in a pretty how town"—its habit of appearing sometimes in standard, sometimes in distinctly nonstandard, syntactic environments.

To appreciate the importance of this aspect of Cummings' technique, we must first restate one interpretively fundamental (and widely accepted) observation about the language of this poem: that the words *anyone* and *noone* have associated with them the personal pronouns *he/him/his* and *she/her* respectively.[29] The appearance of the form *she* in particular leads the reader to suppose a definite female individual (or character) referred to, an assumption which in turn suggests that the "indefinite" member of each pronominal pair may in fact be far from indefinite, constituting a "name," Anyone and Noone respectively. A final logical step dictates that, as is always the case where such anaphoric relationships are found, we can paraphrase constructions in this poem that contain the relevant definite personal pronouns by substituting for each such occurrence the corresponding "name." The clause in line 12 of this poem, for example, "noone loved him more by more," translates by this method to the more fully defined *Noone loved Anyone more by more.* The only aspect of this procedure, as one must apply it to this particular text, that makes it at all remarkable is, of course, that the items used to make the crucial substitutions in this case are themselves pronominal and indeed would normally refer even more vaguely than the (singular personal) pronouns for which they substitute.

This complex situation enables the ironies of Cummings' vision in this poem to emerge with great force. Narratively, after all, it is important that the deep affection of Noone for Anyone should blossom amid the aridity of the uncaring, imperceptive populace of the "pretty how town." The poet himself, however, adds to this apparently simple Romeo-and-Juliet scenario a rather black comic twist, by arranging that both of the contrasted attitudes—the loving and the loveless, the personal and the impersonal—are equally well expressed in the key sentence "noone loved anyone." Radically different interpretations of this simple clause result if we treat the subject and object NPs as proper nouns rather than as indefinite pronouns or *vice versa*. Again in line 26, Cummings mines the same rich vein of ambiguity, where, indeed, I find three rather than only two possible interpretations:

(a) "noone stooped to kiss anyone's face"—with both indefinite pronouns interpreted generically, expressing the continuing emotional bankruptcy of the local population at large;

(b) "noone stooped to kiss Anyone's face"—with Anyone used as a name, to capture the enduring hostility of this community towards the poem's anti-hero; and

(c) "Noone stooped to kiss Anyone's face"—Cummings' reaffirmation of the central theme of his ballad, the love affair of the two named characters.

The importance of being able to substitute *anyone* for *him* and *anyone's* for *his* in this way as a general *interpretive* strategy seems to me irrefutable. What may not have been recognized, I suspect, are the implications of this possibility for the *technical* analysis of the syntactic style of the poem.

If we substitute appropriately for third person singular anaphoric pronouns whenever they occur in this poem, we significantly increase the number of lines in which *anyone* may be said to "occur." In the accompanying table, I list those lines in chronological order, using the letters "A" and "U" to indicate constructions in which the syntactic placement of *anyone* (and that aspect of the syntax alone)

would be ruled acceptable or unacceptable respectively by the rules
of the standard grammar.

This distribution of syntactically acceptable and unacceptable
contexts for the word *anyone* in the poem corresponds strikingly
with the narrative's account of the fluctuating fortunes in love of the
character Anyone.[30] As Anyone's story opens, he is an outsider in the
"pretty how town," an outcast for whom "women and men / cared
. . . not at all." Cummings' syntax early in the poem reflects this
ostracism metaphorically, repeatedly stranding the word *anyone* in
grammatically awkward surroundings, even when this requires, as
we saw earlier, a certain amount of syntactic contortion (". . . loved
anyone not . . ."). The subsequent appearance upon the scene of
noone/Noone (both the word, that is, and the character) provides
anyone/Anyone for the first time with an appropriate linguistic/so-
cial context—a context that then remains intact throughout their
courtship narrated in lines 11–24 of the poem. In line 25, Anyone dies,
his death severing the love-tie that had been his sole point of reference in society. At this point too, appropriately, the acceptability of
anyone as a syntactic constituent again becomes problematical, as it
appears in a nonstandard construction strongly echoic of the opening
words of the poem ("anyone died"). In this case, however, a remedy
for Anyone's isolation is more quickly available in the shape of the
death of Noone (line 26), and as the two protagonists are united in
death, so too the syntax of the poem's closing statements about them
displays a return to harmony by conforming to standard acceptability
judgments.

Any interpretation based on so abstract a syntactic dissection of
this poem might at first seem far-fetched. We should note in passing,
however, that Cummings himself points rather unambiguously to his

(line 1)	anyone lived in a pretty how town	U
(line 4)	anyone sang anyone's didn't	U
	anyone danced anyone's did.	U
(lines 5–6)	Women and men . . .	
	cared for anyone not at all	U
(line 12)	noone loved anyone (more by more)	A
(line 14)	noone laughed anyone's joy	A
	noone cried anyone's grief	A
(line 16)	anyone's any was all to noone	
(line 25)	one day anyone died (i guess)	U
(line 26)	noone stooped to kiss anyone's face	A
(line 31)	noone and anyone . . .	A

own syntactic technique in the text of this poem. In my tabulation of the sentences in the text that contain the word *anyone*, I conspicuously failed to mark line 16 ["anyone's any was all to her (noone)"] as either acceptable or unacceptable. This line poses considerable interpretive problems whatever the critical techniques one is employing. But it is at least somewhat comprehensible if read, so to speak, linguistically rather than narratively, as a syntactic commentary whose implications emerge only in light of Cummings' use of associated syntactic devices elsewhere in the poem. Consider the following sentences, the second probably the most straightforward negation of the first:

> Someone invited all of the guests here tonight.
> Noone invited any of the guests here tonight.

Any in the second of these sentences constitutes the reflex, in a negative context created by the word *noone*, of *all* in the first sentence. Cummings' statement in line 16 of his poem that (to paraphrase for a moment) the *any-* in *anyone* would be the equivalent of *all* to *noone* may thus be read as a linguistic clue to the poem's technical syntactic structure, confirming the important role that syntactic restrictions on the placement of indefinite pronouns play in pressing home one of Cummings' major themes.

The impact of my analysis of "anyone lived in a pretty how town" on the work of stylists such as Levin and Thorne should not be exaggerated. I endorse many of those writers' conclusions; later in this chapter I shall adopt some parts of their respective methods. My own analysis weakens few if any of their assertions about the language of this poem. I certainly accept, for example, Thorne's contention, mentioned earlier, that the sentence *Anyone loved his children* belongs to a stylistically important set of "possible-but-nonoccurring" sentences associated with this poem by the syntactic criteria he describes. I would add to his observation only the suggestion that, if it *had* been used, this sentence would have to have described an unpleasant, unsuccessful, or unfulfilling aspect of Anyone's existence, since the word *anyone* itself appears here in a syntactically nonstandard context as the subject of a positive declarative sentence.

What is significant is that additional insights of this kind more often than not fail to be made at all, since they stem crucially from our having assessed the syntax of this poem by the standards applicable to everyday language, ruling each individual sentence acceptable or unacceptable solely by those standards. Whether he amends the standard grammar with Levin or recasts it with Thorne, the stylist who turns away too fast from the methods that linguists have already devised to account for day-to-day usage will forego the opportunity to crack these particular stylistic codes. Both of the methods that we have examined for adjusting the grammar to explain deviant constructions in poetry accept as "grammatical" *a priori* every one of the poem's attested sentences. Nor will subsequent comparison of the grammar for a particular deviant text with that for standard English remedy the problem. Comparison will demonstrate only the general area in which the poet's rejection of standard practice has introduced a peculiar syntactic flavor to the poem. It will never pinpoint the fact that this rejection may have been undertaken selectively and as a means for reinforcing some such nonlinguistic theme as narrative structure.

The moral to be drawn from this particular example, therefore, is not that there is no place whatsoever for nonstandard rules in stylistic analysis. Rather, I am arguing that a construction which strikes the analyst as nonstandard should *first of all* be assessed in precisely that light, with all the possible relevancies of nonstandard syntactic usage to the poet's purpose being fully explored. Only after this crucial step has been completed should the stylist resort to adaptation or innovation, because both those radical procedures will distort his view of the structure of the text; they will effectively remove all possibility of discriminating between the acceptable and unacceptable constructions since they treat the poem as the only data to be explained, as itself the sole source of propriety judgments.

I have concentrated in the preceding discussion on Levin's and Thorne's analyses of "anyone lived in a pretty how town" as representing two particular schools of technical practice, but the literature abounds in parallel examples. Ann Banfield's work on John Milton's syntactic style seems to me to involve precisely the same procedural limitation.[31] George Dillon's insistence that the lines of poetry that he examines in his early essay "Inversions and Deletions in English Poetry" "do not differ greatly from the output of various optional rules of Modern English,"[32] cannot offset his admission that his general purpose is to describe "*relaxations* of constraints on transformations" that, taken together, "characterize a kind of *extra* syntactic competence required of the reader."[33] Nor does Dillon significantly modify this position in his later monograph, *Language Processing and the Reading of Literature*, where, by shifting the focus of his analysis towards heuristic, highly pragmatic "perceptual strategies," he once more leaves the formal grammar essentially unconstrained, at least as it applies in literary contexts.[34] Even Richard Cureton's admirable approach to the complexities of technical analysis in Cummings' poetry allows the stylist the option of "mak[ing] various minimal changes in the order and substance of the words . . . in order to assign a structural description" to them *before* he has assessed the possibility that "the poet intends to communicate nonsense" or some other notion appropriately expressed in nonstandard syntactic form.[35] In view of this widespread acceptance by stylists of what I take to be mistaken priorities, and their general tolerance for poorly constrained, almost permissive theories in the technical subfield of poetic syntax, perhaps one further textual case study at this point would not be inappropriate.

For this purpose, I turn to "Adonais," Percy Bysshe Shelley's brilliant elegy for John Keats. Three consecutive stanzas of this poem contain lines that, by the standard grammar of English, one would almost certainly want to rule deviant.[36]

Stanza V
And happier they their happiness who knew,
(CWS II, 390:39)

Stanza VI
Thy extreme hope, the loveliest and the last,
The bloom, whose petals nipt before they blew
Died on the promise of the fruit, is waste;
(CWS II, 390: 51–53)

Stanza IV
He died . . .
Blind, old, and lonely, when his country's pride,
The priest, the slave, and the liberticide,
Trampled and mocked with many a loathed rite
Of lust and blood;
(CWS II, 390: 29, 31–34)

We must first take a few moments to pinpoint the source of syntactic infelicity in each of these passages individually. This technical exercise will itself demonstrate among other things the relevance to stylistic analysis of certain concepts at the very forefront of theoretical research in linguistics. Thereafter we may consider the implications of this particular text for the principal topic of discussion in this chapter—the proper treatment of deviant syntax in poetry.

A theoretical syntactician would probably explain the awkwardness that readers sense in line 39 of "Adonais" roughly as follows. Various transformations in English such as *Passivization* may shift syntactic material out of embedded (complement or relative) clauses into higher (or *matrix*) sentences. Thus from the underlying structure (a) in Figure 3, in which *Piglet* is the subject of S2, we can derive by Passivization structure (b), in Figure 4, in which that same NP is the subject of S1.

Structure (a).

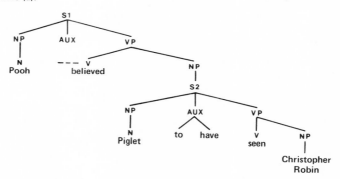

Structure (b).

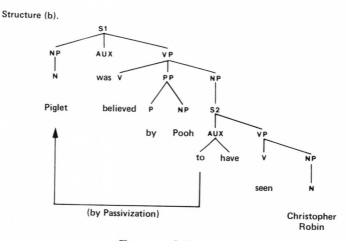

FIG. 3 and FIG. 4

Such movement cannot take place altogether unrestrictedly, however. Any attempt to duplicate this situation when the embedded clause contains a finite verb instead of an infinitive invariably results in an unacceptable derived structure:

> Pooh believed that Piglet had seen Christopher Robin.
> *Piglet was believed by Pooh [S that _____ had seen Christopher Robin].

To account for this restriction, which affects many movement rules besides Passivization, Chomsky has proposed a syntactic constraint, the *Tensed S Condition,* which he formalizes as follows:

> No rule can involve X, Y in the structure
> $$\ldots X \ldots [\alpha \ldots Y \ldots] \ldots$$
> where α is a tensed sentence.[37]

It is well known that not all syntactic rules that move material leftward are subject to this condition in its simplest form.[38] PP-Fronting, for example, can extract syntactic material from finite clauses with considerable freedom:

> Up that path, I could imagine General Wolfe to have climbed at dead of night. (*from* "I could imagine . . . *to have* climbed up that path . . .")

> Up that path, I could imagine General Wolfe had climbed at dead of night. (*from* "I could imagine . . . *had* climbed up that path . . .")

Even for these less heavily restricted transformations, however, cases still exist in which movement is prohibited, as, for example, when the embedded clause is introduced by an overt *complementizer* (roughly what used to be called a relative pronoun or a subordinating conjunction):

> *Up that path I met a man who had climbed. (*from* "I met a man *who* had climbed up that path")

Linguists attribute this secondary restriction to another syntactic condition, the *Doubly-Filled Complementizer Constraint.*[39] Together with the Tensed S Condition and various other constraints, this formal device severely limits the range within which transformations such as PP-Fronting are free to operate.

Let us return now to the relevant line of Shelley's poem:

And happier they their happiness who knew.

It requires no linguistic skills to appreciate that a sentence structurally analogous to this one, such as *Happy is the man his wife who meets (in town),* would appear hopelessly ungrammatical in everyday conversation. The linguist need only study the relationship between Shelley's line and its probable immediately antecedent structure, as shown in Figure 5, to detect the formal reason for this intuitive assessment.

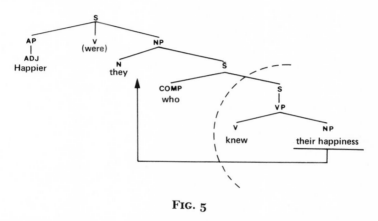

FIG. 5

Whatever the movement rule responsible here for shifting *their happiness* from its underlying position as the post-verbal direct object of *knew* to its location in surface structure immediately before *who,* that rule has clearly applied in violation of the Tensed S Condition, of the Doubly-Filled Complementizer Constraint, or of both at once. As we shall see after I have discussed all three of the passages from "Adonais" relevant to my argument, this violation is by no means insignificant.

George Miller and Noam Chomsky, in an early paper that bears major implications for this whole discussion,[40] detected important limitations on the "depth" of certain types of syntactic structure. Where syntactic complexity is concentrated at the extreme left- or right-hand end of a construction, they noted, our ability to process it syntactically and semantically is limited only by comparatively trivial, nonlinguistic considerations such as the availability of sufficient "space" in our memory:

Left-Branching

[[[[[[Bill's] aunt's] chauffeur's] mistress'] domineering father] mistook Bill for the chauffeur and broke his jaw.]

Right-Branching

[Grumpy mumbled [that Dozy had complained [that it was Snow White's opinion [that the Wicked Queen knew [where they were all living.]]]]]

Where complexity occurs at the center of a given structure, by contrast, our abilities are far more limited. Thus while we accept as complex (but just interpretable) the first sentence below, the second, with only one greater layer of complexity, exceeds our parsing skills altogether (unless we help ourselves by using pen and paper):

Center-Embedded

? [The woman [whom the spider [whose web broke] startled] screamed.]

*[I'll introduce the woman [who [when the spider [whose web broke] startled her] screamed] to my aunt tomorrow.]

In simple terms, this phenomenon is due to the fact that the person who attempts to interpret the first sentence faces the task of processing and memorizing three separate, incomplete syntactic units (*the woman . . ., whom the spider . . .,* and *whose web . . .*). He must then set about retrieving them *in reverse order* so as to match them correctly with their respective predicates, *broke, startled,* and *screamed.* If a retrieval task of this sort is extended beyond three to four or more matched pairs, as in the second sentence, psychologists predict that it will generally defeat us, regardless of the nature of the items to be memorized and recovered—be they numbers, letters, colors, or, as here, syntactic constituents. Our discomfort with such center-embedded syntactic structures thus represents merely a special case of a rather general limitation on our innate cognitive powers.

In light of the preceding discussion, we may now return to some lines quoted earlier from Stanza VI of "Adonais." I repeat the passage below, inserting the relevant syntactic bracketing:

> [Thy extreme hope, the loveliest and the last,
> The bloom, [whose petals [nipt [before they blew]]
> Died on the promise of the fruit,] is waste.]

It should now be clear where we must lay the blame for the intuitively obvious complexity of these lines. Shelley's syntax here displays a classically center-embedded form and inevitably places an inordinate and quite perceptible strain on the reader's language-processing capabilities by violating this crucial constraint.

The *Center-Embedding Constraint,* the Tensed S Condition, and the Doubly-Filled Complementizer Constraint have all been extensively analyzed by theoretical linguists. Less thoroughly explored is a constraint that explains, I believe, our uneasiness in reading Stanza IV of "Adonais." At issue here is language's inbuilt resistance to allowing nonstandard stylistic processes to add to the already heavy burden of potential ambiguity that inheres in syntactic surface structures. The basic insight was, once again, Chomsky's:

> [S]tylistic inversion . . . is tolerated up to ambiguity—that is, up to the point where a structure is produced that might have been generated independently by [other] grammatical rules.[41]

Banfield picked up on Chomsky's lead in her dissertation, suggesting more concretely that, beyond the critical "point" that he had described, a syntactic condition (which I shall call the *Up-to-Ambiguity Condition*) actually prevented the generation of surface structures whose form might be attributed with equal plausibility to either of two syntactic processes.[42]

English syntax permits leftward movement of simple NPs under various circumstances. Perhaps the simplest such case is *Topicalization,* which preposes a specified NP to sentence-initial position (see Figure 6). The surface word order that results from this operation, it may be noted, is object (O), followed by subject (S), then verb (V). Such sentences are reasonably common in everyday as well as in poetic language. But any account of syntactic practices in English

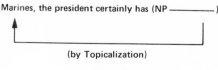

Marines, the president certainly has (NP —————)

(by Topicalization)

FIG. 6

poetry will have to account in addition for sentences whose surface structures display an SOV configuration, as in the following lines:

> And when we meet at any time again,
> Be it not seen in either of our brows
> That (NP *we*) (NP *one jot of former love*) retain.
> (Michael Drayton, "Since there's no help . . .," lines 6–8; my
> emphases)

In his paper on poetic inversion, Dillon makes a strong case for assuming that this configuration results from application of a stylistic rule of *Verb Final*, but he also astutely remarks that that rule is considerably complicated by the fact that "the position of the verb is normally crucial for determining grammatical relations."[43] Since the Verb Final transformation evades both of the standard SVO and OSV word orders by substituting an SOV surface structure, he notes in particular, the grammar places various additional *ad hoc* restrictions on the operation of that rule to ensure that overall complexity is kept to a minimum. (No *additional* dislocatory rules, for instance, seem able to apply once Verb Final has been selected.)

Of immediate interest to us is the closely related observation that the respective outputs of Topicalization and of Verb Final will often appear sufficiently similar to fall within the scope of the Up-to-Ambiguity Condition. We may take lines 32–34 of "Adonais" as a perfect case in point. *Trampled* and *mocked* being transitive verbs, the reader must try to determine which of the NPs preceding them is the subject and which is the object:

> . . . when [NP1 *his country's pride,*]
> [NP2 *The priest, the slave, and the liberticide,*]
>   Trampled and mocked . . .

Has NP1 here been moved from object position by Topicalization? Or were the conjoined verbs moved to clause-final position by Verb Final, leaving NP1 and NP2 in their original deep-structure (S-O) order? The task of solving this problem—which is made no easier in practice, certainly, by Shelley's prolific use of commas which mislead the reader into wondering whether NP2 might not even be appositive to NP1—cannot be accomplished if one relies on syntactic evidence alone. Only by semantic criteria, and even then only if he already knows of Shelley's enduring political·opposition to the more conservative and authoritarian elements of the British church and state, can the reader disentangle the structure of this passage correctly. (In actual fact, NP2 is the subject of the sentence, NP1 having indeed been fronted by Topicalization.) The problems that we experience in successfully determining the structure of this stanza of the poem are thus precisely those that the Up-to-Ambiguity Condition is supposed to preclude.[44]

At first glance, the technical sketch that I have attempted in the preceding paragraphs may appear rather dry. Three consecutive stanzas of Shelley's "Adonais," I have argued, contain sentences that violate simple but supposedly absolute constraints on English syntactic processes; as a result, they strike the reader as unusual or awkward. Stated in this way, the analysis seems positively routine. Yet its implications for stylistic methods in general are by no means trivial, and involve both the issue of which linguistic model a stylist should work with and the question of what his priorities should be in conducting his technical analysis. We may summarize the most important points as follows.

(a) *It is essential that the technical analysis of poetic syntax be conducted using the most modern linguistic methods available.* Earlier in this chapter, I discussed this claim from a theoretical standpoint; I now reaffirm it for entirely practical reasons. The all-important link just uncovered among the three passages quoted from "Adonais" could never have been isolated had I not been employing a technical framework that recognized the existence of both syntactic transformations, and, more particularly still, conditions governing their operation. Such concepts have been developed within linguistic theory itself only quite recently. They thus demonstrate well the need for stylists to stay abreast of even the most current advances in linguistic science.

(b) *Even purely technical analyses, stylistic accounts that contain absolutely no interpretation of the passages they describe, may nevertheless interest and assist the literary scholar.* In the present instance, for example, my conclusions could be used to add focus and definition [not to mention objective support—see point (c) below] to previous commentators' essentially intuitive and subjective remarks about Shelley's use of the English language.

Shelley's style in general has often come under critical fire for its "syntactic disorders."[45] Remarks on this aspect of his work have varied in their specificity. Deborah Rosenfelt, in fact, came quite close to identifying syntactically at least those problems that we would now attribute to Shelley's reliance on center-embedded constructions; she complained that his poetry too often exhibited "lengthy interruptions in the main line of the sentence."[46] But the usefulness even of comments about Shelley's poetic style as insightful and precisely stated as this one has been seriously compromised by the fact that their technical basis has generally been insufficiently sophisticated. The "length" of the "interruptions," we now realize in particular, is far less important than their structural location and their overall "depth."

Armed with this new information, the stylist may move forward without fearing repeated challenges to his basic technical premises. Such additional research might for example take the form of comparing Shelley's syntactic complexity with that of Milton or Cummings.

(c)   *Not all technical features isolated by stylistic analysis are mere reflections of the analyst's preconceived notions of what should (interpretively speaking) be the major emphases within the text.* This is a charge repeatedly leveled by Barbara Herrnstein Smith and by Stanley Fish, who accuse stylists of maintaining the naive belief that there exist some "formal features that one can pick out independently of any interpretation of them."[47] Any such pretense of separating technical from interpretive judgments, Fish maintains, is either downright dishonest or self-deluding.

The present case, I suggest, disproves his claim. Whether or not a given syntactic structure within "Adonais" is center-embedded or violates the Doubly-Filled Complementizer Constraint is a factual issue, altogether unaffected by the interpretations that a stylist may subsequently decide to place upon it. No competing derivations, no shadings or revisions of the grammar are involved here; the issue is, for once, black and white.

Indeed, I might well go further and argue that even a statement about readers' responses to these constraint violations could well remain objective and noninterpretive. Linguists have claimed increasingly often in the past decade that the existence of syntactic conditions at all and even certain aspects of their

formal shape might be determined by cognitive strategies relied
on by hearers and readers for interpreting sentences.[48] To over-
simplify the argument for a moment, it is suggested that all
syntactic constraints may exist to ensure that surface structures
generated by the grammar do not positively mislead the lan-
guage-analyzer in our heads as it goes about its task of decoding
sentences.

Within such a framework, we may note, a poet's decision to
violate a given condition *necessarily* puts the reader's mind
under a certain kind of cognitive pressure.[49] To assess the relevance of this fact to our understanding of the text as a whole
represents by all means an interpretive act; but simply recognizing it *as* a fact involves us only in an empirical claim within the
technical field, a claim certainly subject to subsequent confirmation or disproof.

All three of these conclusions constitute useful substantiation for
claims I advanced earlier in this study. Equally significant, though,
is the fact that my technical analysis of these lines from "Adonais"
provides important confirmation for a fourth point I made in the
immediately preceding portion of this chapter about preferred
strategies for describing deviant syntactic constructions in poetic
texts:

(d) *Stylistic insights may be lost wherever technical analysis pro-
ceeds with the principal aim of showing how all lines of a given
text may be encompassed (ruled acceptable) by a custom-
designed poetic syntax.* On the one hand, it is unclear, given all
that has been said about syntactic conditions above, how a stylist's specialized grammar for a text such as "Adonais" *could*
arbitrarily rule fully acceptable a series of structures which, linguists would maintain, our cognitive faculties simply fail adequately to process. Such an exercise in futility would reduce the
stylist's accountability to linguistic theory to zero and enclose the
technical analysis of poetic syntax within a hermetically sealed
bubble.

On the other hand, a "grammar-fixing" approach to the
opening section of "Adonais" would also, presumably, have to
proceed by assuming Shelley's style in that poem to be *uni-*

formly unheedful of syntactic conditions and constraints. The conditions in question would, in effect, be struck altogether from the grammar formulated for this poem. This approach unfortunately overlooks a crucial, uneven distribution of syntactic deviations in this text. It turns out that *only* Stanzas IV, V, and VI of the poem contain such marked syntactic aberrations (a fact which is highly significant, as I shall show in detail when I return in chapter 4 to a discussion of how we set about interpreting this elegy). But a stylistic analysis that reacts to each violation merely by recasting the grammar for this poem by deleting the relevant constraint altogether loses thereby its sensitivity to the presence or absence of similar violations elsewhere in the text.

As in the discussion of Cummings' "anyone lived in a pretty how town," so too here we discover the danger caused by premature capitulation to the temptation to rule-monger. Discriminating the acceptable from the unacceptable within a single text becomes impossible unless deviations are treated as precisely that. Only reluctantly, then, if at all, should the analyst move away from the standard grammar in the direction of a more powerful, less restricted syntax for his text.

IV

The act of stepping outside the standard grammar to complete a technical stylistic analysis is itself fraught with various theoretical and practical dangers. From the very beginning of modern stylistic research, the vast power of transformational grammars again loomed as the major obstacle to uncontroversial analyses; a deviant syntactic construction, far from lacking any adequate formal account, usually admitted of several. Naturally, therefore, if a little sluggishly, stylists began the search for suitable criteria by which to judge the relative merits of competing technical analyses.

Perhaps the most popular such criterion—he calls it a "methodological moral"—is that advocated by Dillon:

> [O]ne should assume the minimum of difference between poetic syntax and that of ordinary language.[50]

As we have already seen, Levin would almost certainly endorse this recommendation and in this particular respect would find a strong ally in Thorne:

> [T]here will be a tendency to make the grammar of the literary dialect as nearly isomorphic with the grammar of the language . . . as possible.[51]

For a long time, the terms "different" and "isomorphic," clearly vital to an adequate assessment of this principle, went completely undefined, as did the methodological steps by which one should proceed if one wished to discover in practice the maximally "similar" syntactic account desired. John Lipski justly complained in 1977 that seldom in the literature did one "find explicit criteria for establishing the transitions necessary" to define a stylistic grammar on this principle.[52] Within this context, Cureton's 1980 dissertation represented a major breakthrough, making a number of highly significant contributions toward remedying this deficiency in the technical subfield of stylistic theory. For those interested in a clearer understanding of the principle of isomorphism, I strongly recommend chapter 3 of that valuable work.

Vital as such studies may be, I wish to plot a somewhat different course. It seems to me by no means a foregone conclusion that isomorphism with the standard grammar, however that may ultimately be defined, should in fact constitute our primary goal in describing poetic syntax. As a syntactician, I find it most disturbing that such a principle, based as it is on the *external* orientation of the grammar proposed, should have been adopted as a methodological *a priori*. In recent linguistic theory, by contrast, the assumption has generally been that analysts' efforts will be directed initially towards establishing a range of individual grammars on the basis of purely *internal* criteria of adequacy. Only after a number of such grammars have achieved a substantial measure of descriptive power in their own right does the linguist induce any generalizations about properties that those grammars may have in common. Thus, for instance, virtually every attempt to establish so-called linguistic universals has grown out of, rather than preceded, detailed investigation of a number of specific natural languages. Only in this way, it is felt, can the theory being developed avoid the trap of becoming self-defeatingly prescriptive.

My thesis in the discussion that follows, then, will be that, in designing a syntactic model for stylistically deviant language, the need *to reflect major syntactic generalizations* about the language of a given text should claim the stylist's attention above and beyond all other methodological considerations. In adopting this position, I shall, in a sense, be accepting the basic philosophy of Thorne's paper as cited earlier in this chapter, advocating with him that each text be treated as a separate block of data demanding a maximally simple and elegant account of its own idiosyncratic regularities. I shall differ from him only in rejecting his essentially unsupported assumption that the most descriptively adequate account of a text within this framework may be determined equally effectively simply by demanding isomorphism with the standard grammar. To take another point of reference, I shall bypass Dillon's first "methodological moral," which I quoted earlier, in favor of a second, which he advances almost as an afterthought: "that one must consider the grammar of the poet *as a whole.*"[53]

If one were interested in elaborating what Dillon at one point calls "a taxonomy of difficulty" in the works of various English poets,[54] one might contrast the syntactic complexity of Shelley's style with that found in the poetry of Alexander Pope, which may be attributed not to any violation of syntactic conditions or constraints, but to the many coordinate sentence structures in his poems from which constituents have been deleted by processes unacceptable in the standard language.[55] The following examples are typical:[56]

While Fish in Streams, or Birds delight in Air,
("The Rape of the Lock": PAP, 231: 163)

Who writes a Libel, or who copies out:
("Epistle to Dr. Arbuthnot": PAP, 607: 290)

Favours to none, to all she Smiles extends,
("The Rape of the Lock": PAP, 223: 11)

The material deleted from each of these lines can, of course, be inferred by the reader upon reflection. He can, that is, reconstruct the presumably underlying clausal structures:

While Fish *delight* in Streams, (. . .)
(. . .) or who copies out *a Libel,*

and

She extends Favours to none, (. . .).

Still, precisely analogous surface structures in everyday contexts would, as I shall shortly demonstrate in detail, be judged unacceptable. Thus the stylist is faced with the task of accounting technically for the success of a series of structures not explicable within the framework of the standard grammar.

Furthermore, constructions of the kind cited in the preceding paragraph pervade Pope's poetry. As a result of such widespread occurrence, they cannot be expected to correlate with specific themes that might then justify positing *strategically* confused or ungrammatical syntactic expression of the kind we discussed in connection with Cummings and Shelley above. Tentatively, therefore, we may begin instead to explore ways of extending the syntax of standard English so that it will actually generate such examples, watching at the same time for means by which we might ultimately evaluate each such formal extension as a more or less desirable contribution toward a custom-designed grammar of Pope's poetry.

Let us begin this exploration by analyzing line 163 of "The Rape of the Lock," considering in turn two possible technical accounts of the surface form it manifests. Let us assume, first, that deviant structures in poetic texts always bear maximally "transparent" relations to their deep-structure sources.[57] This hypothesis will lead us to assign line 163 some such underlying structure as that in Figure 7.

Deriving line 163 as it actually appears in the text of the poem

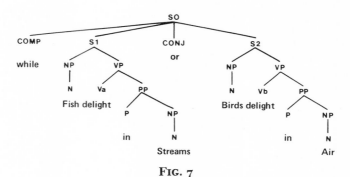

FIG. 7

from such a deep structure will require that we delete Va *(delight)* from the left conjunct, presumably on the basis of its identity with the corresponding verb in the structurally parallel right conjunct. Generally speaking, such an approach would not represent a particularly extreme proposal. Coordinate structure deletions of this kind are common in English as in many other languages, and the specific process involved here, usually termed *Gapping*, has generated extensive theoretical discussion among linguists as a *bona fide* transformation in the standard grammar.[58] One aspect of Pope's application of the Gapping rule in this particular context does, however, demand further comment. In standard English, Gapping deletes material from the right and not the left of two parallel conjuncts, as can be clearly seen from the following sentences:

Pope lived near London and Swift lived in Ireland.
Pope lived near London and Swift, _____ in Ireland.
* Pope _____ near London and Swift lived in Ireland.

The sentence that Pope employs in his poem, of course, conforms precisely to the usually *unacceptable* pattern illustrated in the third of these sentences. Were we to adopt the general approach to the technical analysis of this passage that I have just outlined, therefore, we would have to take the important step of extending the grammar of standard English so as to permit leftward or "backward" Gapping.

At this point I want briefly to set alongside this technical analysis of line 163 a second, initially plausible, approach, but one which we shall eventually find evidence to reject. This second approach would abandon the deep structure for this sentence given above in favor of a more abstract one in which S2 preceded rather than followed S1 (as in Figure 8). Gapping can of course apply to *this* structure in a perfectly straightforward, left-to-right manner, correctly deleting *delight* from S1. Now, however, we shall have to posit a new rule of

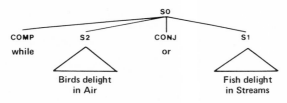

FIG. 8

Conjunct Scrambling to account for the fact that, in surface structure, S1 appears to the left of S2. While simple enough to devise, such a rule is nonstandard, and its addition represents the "cost" of this second approach to the overall economy of the grammar being proposed.

Our discussion thus far has led us to formulate two hypotheses concerning the derivation of our problematical line from "The Rape of the Lock."[59] Each involves making a single clearly delimited adjustment to some aspect of standard English syntax. Under the first hypothesis, it will be necessary to apply the Gapping transformation backward; the formal statement of that rule will therefore have to be altered accordingly. In the second, we shall need instead to introduce a completely new rule, Conjunct Scrambling, to ensure the correct surface order of the coordinate clauses involved. It is extremely important to remember also that any decision we make to prefer one of these hypotheses over the other will do far more than just provide a preferred technical account of one line. It will affect the treatment of numerous parallel cases in Pope's poetry, of which the following are merely a representative sample:

> Now Leaves the Trees, and Flow'rs adorn the Ground;
> ("Pastorals: Spring": PAP, 125: 43)

> Some few in *that,* but Numbers err in *this,*
> ("Essay on Criticism": PAP, 144: 5)

> A Belt her Waste, a Fillet binds her Hair,
> ("Windsor-Forest": PAP, 201: 178)

We should therefore proceed with some caution when determining what would constitute legitimate arguments in favor of one or the other of our two hypotheses.

Early evidence on the side of what we could call the "Conjunct Scrambling Hypothesis" might include the observation that not all of the examples of irregular coordinate structure deletion in Pope's work involve just two conjoined clauses; in several instances, deletion results in far more obviously "scrambled" patterns. Let us briefly return, for example, to line 163 of "The Rape of the Lock." That line, we now see, constitutes only the first part of a construction that as a whole spans two lines, a construction in which *delight* has been deleted from the third, as well as from the first, of three conjuncts:

While Fish _____ in Streams, or Birds delight in Air,
Or in a Coach and Six _____ the *British* Fair,
(PAP, 231: 163–164)

It is thus in actual fact the verb of a *medial* clause that apparently controls two deletions (one leftward and the other rightward) in this passage. Nor does this pattern represent the only possibility even where just three clauses are involved. In my next example, deletion sites occur in clauses one and two, the verb *supply* (and incidentally the direct object *him*, also missing in the earlier clauses) appearing only in the third conjunct:

Happy the man, . . .
Whose herds with milk, whose fields with bread,
Whose flocks supply him with attire,
("Ode on Solitude": PAP, 265: 1, 5–6)

And a similar case from Pope's "Epistle to Cobham" exhibits a still more complex distribution of deletions, with the only overt mention of the crucial verb *turn* appearing in the *second* of *four* conjoined clauses:

Manners with Fortunes, Humours turn with Climes,
Tenets with Books, and Principles with Times.
(PAP, 555: 166–167)

It might well be argued that in such cases uniform rightward application of Gapping, to be followed by fairly random scrambling of the various clauses involved, represents the elegant derivational path. By comparison, simultaneous forward *and* backward Gapping of the kind that would be required within an extended grammar that had no scrambling rule looks distinctly clumsy.

Against such formal syntactic arguments in favor of the conjunct scrambling solution one must weigh reasons of an altogether different kind for preferring the "Backward Gapping Hypothesis." Suppose, for example, that we adopt temporarily the assumption that the preferred stylistic grammar should always be the one that generates the smallest possible set of nonstandard sentences beyond those already contained in the text under examination. (While almost impossible to realize in terms of "hard" statistics, such a doctrine has at least the distinct merit of providing an explicit, theoretically quantifiable criterion for measuring stylistic isomorphism.) In the present case, Conjunct Scrambling will potentially apply to a very wide range of coordinate structures. Indeed, unless carefully constrained, its addition to the grammar will make extremely difficult the task of determining unambiguously the precise deep-structure order of *any* pair of conjoined clauses. Permitting backward Gapping, by contrast, will affect only a subset of conjoined clauses, those that display strict structural congruity and a certain degree of local referential identity.[60] By this standard, therefore, the Backward Gapping Hypothesis emerges as the preferred, because the more restrictive, account of Pope's poetic syntax.

Neither of these arguments, though, strikes me as irrefutable. Calculating the potential of some rule for generating nonstandard sentences represents only one possible scale on which to measure isomorphism with the standard grammar; the total number of rules added or dropped or the overall "naturalness" of the new grammar might be equally plausibly proposed. In any case, the theoretical cost of introducing a rule such as Conjunct Scrambling could only be finally assessed in light of its usefulness both here *and elsewhere* in accounting for stylistic phenomena in Pope's works. In the end, such a debate is not so much unresolvable in my view as irrelevant, the whole picture being altered fundamentally by the observation that there exists a *second* class of nonstandard coordinate surface structures in Pope's works.

A representative member of this second class, contained in a line from "The Epistle to Dr. Arbuthnot," was cited earlier in this discussion:

Who writes a Libel, or who copies out.

Copy out, a transitive verb, appears in this line without a specified direct object. As the context makes perfectly clear, that object must in deep structure have been identical to the object NP of the syntactically parallel preceding clause, *a Libel,* yet deletion from such a configuration is never admissible in the standard language:

*The man who loves his wife and who respects ____ should be universally admired.

A pronominal object *(her)* must appear in the second clause if the whole construction is to be judged acceptable. Not that English never permits the deletion under identity of rightmost constituents in conjoined clauses. Indeed, where the item to be deleted is the rightmost constituent of a *lefthand* conjunct, as in sentence (b) below, deletion is highly probable. Only where the deletion works from left to right are problems encountered, as illustrated in sentence (c).

(a) Nixon made the tapes, and Miss Woods erased the tapes.
(b) Nixon made ____ _____, and Miss Woods erased, the tapes.
(c)* Nixon made the tapes, and Miss Woods erased ____ _____.

The transformation that derives the acceptable (b) sentence here, usually referred to as *Right Node Raising,* has never to my knowledge been satisfactorily described in formal terms. Its various properties, however, have been closely examined and its characteristic proscription of rightward deletion noted.[61] What, then, are we to make of Pope's line in his "Epistle," where it is the supposedly illegal option that the poet has evidently invoked?

One approach would be simply to adjust the standard syntax by relaxing the prohibition on rightward Right Node Raising. This would permit an intuitively direct derivation to connect the attested sentence with the plausible deep-structure source shown in the tree-structure in Figure 9. It would also require, however, that we effectively double the potential output of the Right Node Raising transformation by allowing it to apply freely in either direction.

An altogether different approach would again involve use of the Conjunct Scrambling rule and would indeed closely parallel that proposed for Gapping cases in the preceding section of this argu-

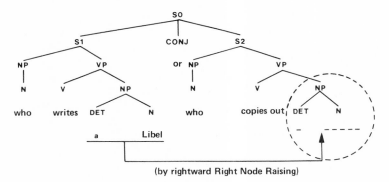

(by rightward Right Node Raising)

FIG. 9

ment. S2, that is, would be generated before S1 in deep structure; the direct object of *copies out* would be deleted by standard (leftward) Right Node Raising; and Conjunct Scrambling would finally invert S1 and S2 to yield the attested line. At first glance, certainly, this second approach appears quite elegant, especially in view of the possibility discussed earlier that Conjunct Scrambling might be included in our syntax for Pope's poetry on independent grounds—the need to handle cases of apparent backward Gapping.

Any premature hopes, however, that the Conjunct Scrambling Hypothesis might offer an integrated solution to all of the coordinate structure deletion irregularities encountered so far are promptly dashed when one comes to consider the following line from Pope's "Essay on Man":

Since but to wish more Virtue, is to gain.
(PAP, 545: 326)

We find here a construction involving two sentences that behave, at least from the point of view of syntactic deletion, very much like a pair of conjoined clauses. The matrix sentence in this case is, however, copular, and semantically the sentence as a whole connects the two clauses in a virtual cause-and-effect relationship. To posit in this case an underlying sentence

To gain more virtue is but to wish more virtue,

as the Conjunct Scrambling Hypothesis would dictate, appears radically counterintuitive. Worse yet, such a step would grant Conjunct Scrambling enormous latitude, permitting it to reverse fundamental semantic predications and compounding the problems noted earlier that are created by this rule for the unambiguous determination of underlying syntactic structure. Once again, then, we appear to be faced with two equally imperfect hypotheses to describe a specific set of nonstandard constructions.[62]

Let us pause a moment to take stock of our position. We began this section of the chapter by studying constructions in Pope's poetry in which the results of syntactic deletion most closely resembled those usually associated with the Gapping transformation. We noted, however, that the particular sentences Pope wrote were nonstandard in that deletion occurred in the left- rather than the right-hand conjunct. Two formal descriptions of this situation (the Conjunct Scrambling Hypothesis and the Backward Gapping Hypothesis) seemed equally plausible *prima facie*. We then turned to cases in which deletion appeared to have resulted from some form of Right Node Raising.[63] Again we encountered irregularities and were forced to consider various means of accounting for them. Conjunct Scrambling, on this occasion, proved unable to account for at least one important case, in which the copular verb *be* rather than a conjunction linked the relevant clauses in a nonreversible semantic predication. In the case of this second class of examples, I now want to stress, only one formal extension of the grammar could effectively handle all of the examples that I adduced. Only one, that is to say, which we might call the "Rightward Right Node Raising Hypothesis," achieved even "observational adequacy" on Chomsky's hierarchy of theoretical adequacy.[64] At one level, of course, this discovery allows us to assert a firm preference for the Rightward Right Node Raising Hypothesis where that hypothesis is in fact directly applicable. At another level, though, the same result may be brought to bear on the parallel and more delicately balanced problems of how to approach cases of apparent backward Gapping in Pope's poetry.

Evidence in this area, it will be recalled, seemed inconclusive when discussion was confined solely to the lines with Gapping-style deletion patterns. Now, however, from a broader perspective, we can see that the situation is far less uncertain. Both Right Node Raising and Gapping may be classified as coordinate structure deletion transformations. Both share significant characteristics and restrictions on their operation. If, therefore, we accept both *rightward* Right Node Raising and *backward* Gapping as the appropriate ways in which to account for their respective classes of nonstandard constructions in Pope's poetry, then we shall be able to infer an important higher-level generalization about Pope's syntactic style: *that Pope characteristically applies coordinate structure deletion transformations without regard to any restrictions imposed on the direction in which they may operate by the syntax of the standard language.*

It is to this end that my whole discussion in the preceding pages has tended. I have sought a formal description of Pope's syntactic deviance that could stand, as any linguistic hypothesis should stand, the requirement that it characterize "significant generalizations about the structure" of the data it purports to describe.[65] Such a requirement appears to me altogether crucial to the proper technical analysis of poetic style. In some cases, perhaps in many, the syntactic choices that it dictates will indeed conform to those that would result from applying Thorne's doctrine of maximal isomorphism with the standard grammar. But where these two methodological morals conflict, I maintain that there can be no doubt which should be the stylist's "Golden Rule."

V

Despite the length and detail of the three discussions that have occupied the greater part of this chapter, I have only begun to explore a daunting mass of material in the subfield of technical analysis that stylists urgently need to consider. Listing all the material *not* discussed would of course be futile, but we may usefully consider for a moment just a few of the other broad subject areas that await adequate treatment:

(a)   How should stylistics approach texts in which no deviant syntactic constructions as such occur but in which at the same time unusually heavy usage of a particular syntactic process (or group of allied processes) results in a unique stylistic flavor?[66]

(b)   What relationship, if any, obtains between the methods of technical stylistics and those used in other branches of so-called applied linguistics? Can all nonstandard dialects, whether literary, geographical, or social, be handled according to the same principles of analysis?

(c)   More generally still, what can the theoretical syntactician himself learn from the ways in which poetic syntax differs from that of the standard language? Can evidence from poetic practice be used to support one hypothesis about the standard language over another?

All these, like the issues discussed (however inadequately) in the course of this chapter, are empirical questions. They are also, to be sure, complex and elusive. The theoretical conclusions to which they may lead us, however, are by no means trivial. The careful and accurate formulation of a technical analysis of each individual work offers the beleaguered discipline of stylistics its best shot at general credibility; and "accuracy" in matters such as these is inseparable from thoughtful and closely reasoned discussion of proper procedures by which to derive those analyses. Harold Whitehall's assertion that "no criticism can go beyond its linguistics"[67] is clearly too strong, too territorially aggressive; the corollary that "no stylistics can survive poor linguistics" is by contrast one that every stylist would do well to take to heart.

CHAPTER | **The Aesthetic**

THREE | **Dimension**

I

I often find surprising the weight that some stylists are willing to lay on technical evidence that has been reduced to quantitative or statistical summary. Some issues certainly respond well to statistical investigation—decisions about how to attribute literary works, for example, about authenticating newly discovered correspondence, or about dating historical fragments. But the general reader should beware whenever a stylist combines an explication of this particular specialization with the chauvinistic claim that that branch of stylistics (itself only a subspecialty, it seems to me, within technical analysis) represents all that is worthy of attention in this marvelously fertile discipline.

Typical of such a claim would be the assertion that "[when] authors opt for the same transformations, their styles are said to be similar."[1] In this chapter, I hope to show, to the contrary, that if we seek a concept of style that will be easily recognized by the general reader, our own researches will have to range considerably more widely. A mere count of rule applications may satisfactorily "fingerprint an author,"[2] but to claim that it reveals all that needs to be considered in a stylistic analysis is surely to indulge in the critical equivalent of palmistry.[3] In the pages that follow, I shall illustrate how notions such as "similar" and "different" can depend on aspects of syntactic form widely divorced even from *less* quantitatively rigid technical analysis, and I shall introduce a second class of statements about style which will begin to give us the flexibility that the narrowly technical approach so obviously denies.

In John Dryden's elegiac ode "To the Pious Memory of . . . Mrs. Anne Killigrew" we find the lines:[4]

> The Sacred Poets first shall hear the Sound, . . .
> And streight, with in-born Vigour, on the Wing,
> Like mounting Larkes, to the New Morning sing.
> (WJD III, 115: 188, 191–192)

These striking lines occur as this poem reaches its extraordinary emotional climax. In them, Dryden seeks not only to convey to his readers his vision of Anne Killigrew's apotheosis as a "Harbinger of Heav'n" (line 194), but also to express the intensity of his personal commitment to that vision, a double focus referred to by the editors of WJD as Dryden's combination of "irrepressible lyricism and fervent conviction" (WJD III, 317). A review of the syntactic structure of this passage reveals one of several ways in which Dryden achieves the second of his two ambitious goals, injecting an air of excitement and fervency into the narration of these altogether mythical events.

Underlying lines 191–192 of this poem a transformational syntactician would in all probability posit something like this deep structure:

> (The sacred poets shall) straight sing to the new morning with inborn vigor like mounting larks on the wing.

The four PPs in this clause would all, that is, be generated underlyingly at the righthand end of their dominating VP. Their eventual position in Dryden's surface structure would be attributed to a subsequent wholesale application of PP-Fronting. But such remarks about the technical background of this particular passage are of little interest when compared with other comments that one may make about the surface configuration itself. For what surely strikes the reader most forcibly about the linguistic form of this couplet is that, by distorting the underlying word order, Dryden delays for nineteen syllables (almost the full two lines of verse available) his revelation of what exactly the "Sacred Poets . . . shall" *do* on the Judgment Day.

Let us for a moment trace the steps of the reader as he encounters this passage and attempts to analyze it for the first time.[5] He must first read and file away, so to speak, the subject and auxiliary verb of this clause (*Poets* and *shall* respectively). After completing work on the first of its conjoined predicates, which is, as it happens, comparatively straightforward, he reaches the second (. . . *and streight* . . .). At this point, however, he must continue to hold in abeyance both subject and auxiliary while he interprets the four increasingly evocative preposed PPs, for only after he has negotiated these obstacles will Dryden finally grant him the all-important verb, *sing.* The culminative force that this small word carries is due in part, no doubt, to its metrical and phonological role in completing the *wing/sing* rhyme, and in part to the fact that it suddenly clarifies semantically the relevance of the prominent simile of the "mounting Larkes." Just as important, though, is the fact that *sing* resolves the suspended syntactic structure of this second VP, the effectiveness of this resolution being heightened by the sheer length of the preceding delay.[6]

Two problems arise if one tries to describe the temporary frustration experienced in reading this couplet simply as a technical syntactic phenomenon. First, transformational grammarians have arbitrarily ruled such matters outside the domain of theoretical linguistics. Were the interruption to the forward progress of interpretation at this point itself a center-embedded construction and thus, as we saw in the course of our discussion of Shelley's style, liable to halt parsing altogether, the syntactician might show some interest. If, alternatively, that same material were to encourage *premature* (and false) parsing by providing constituents capable of being accidentally misanalyzed as the predicate to "Sacred Poets . . . shall," a psycholinguist at least might have relevant observations to make about it as a kind of syntactic "garden path" sentence.[7] In general, however, matters involving linguistic memory and its limitations have consistently been viewed as facets of linguistic *performance* and virtually excluded from serious theoretical study.[8]

In itself, this first obstacle to integrating the concept of syntactic delay into technical stylistic analysis is largely procedural. Liberalizing the definition of syntactic competence to include such factors could be easily accomplished and might well prove beneficial. But there remains a second, altogether more significant, reason for avoiding this innovation. Consider in this connection a second textual example. Lines 77–98 of George Gordon, Lord Byron's "Childish

Recollections" seem at first to flow from the pen of a contrite poet
ashamed of his early "childish" vituperations:[9]

> Away with themes like this! not mine the task
> From flattering friends to tear the hateful mask; . . .
> Or, if my muse a pedant's portrait drew,
> POMPOSUS' virtues are but known to few:
> (BPW, 34: 77–78, 89–90)

Leavening this rather stodgy and self-righteous fare the reader is
delighted to find flashes of temper that show Byron's more characteristic reluctance to capitulate without putting up a good fight. Lines
91–92 in particular betray just such a strong sense of assertive indig-
nation:

> I never fear'd the young usurper's nod,
> And he who wields must sometimes feel the rod.
> (BPW, 34: 91–92)

In the bland context just described, the rod, as archetypal symbol of
just, even divine, chastisement, stands out boldly. As in the passage
from Dryden's elegy discussed previously, the concomitant stylistic
prominence of the *word* "rod" is supported in part by Byron's exploitation of the rhyme-slot in the second line of the couplet. Again as
in the earlier case, however, this culminative constituent also completes a syntactic construction that had been left hanging, object-less,
in mid-line ("and he who wields . . .").

In both these passages, then, poets achieve stylistic emphasis by
creating a syntactic distance between parts of a single construction,
temporarily suspending or delaying the reader's ability to parse the
language of the text before him. Yet—and this is the most important
observation of all—Byron's *technical* method in his couplet differs
radically from Dryden's in the lines from the Killigrew ode. Where
Dryden, as we saw, used PP-Fronting, a movement rule, to *interpose*
syntactic material between his subject and its verb, Byron employs
Right Node Raising simply to *delete* what would otherwise have been
the first occurrence of *rod*, postponing until the second any chance
for a complete interpretation of either conjunct (see Figure 10). Any
technical analysis of these two passages, then, will inevitably and
quite properly concentrate on isolating, in linguistic terms, this important *difference* between their styles. The contrapuntal *similarity*

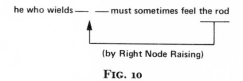

(by Right Node Raising)

FIG. 10

that we detect between them despite their technical disparity would seem to be of an altogether different order, directly related to syntactic structure by all means, but encompassing also nonsyntactic factors such as distance (or delay) and suspension. It will be the general aim of this chapter to explore further the definition and application of such concepts in literary criticism—concepts which I categorize under the heading "aesthetic."[10]

II

Richard Cureton undertakes in his dissertation "to present, illustrate, and document a typology of syntactic *aesthetic* effects,"[11] a step which, he claims, will permit stylists to break out of their blinkered commitment to either highly formalistic, interpretively contentless linguistics or technically sloppy, albeit insightful, literary criticism. As my remarks throughout the preceding pages should have made clear, I strongly sympathize with Cureton's general goal. When his "typology" itself arrives, furthermore, I find it disappointing only in that Cureton repeatedly uses the single term "aesthetic" to cover altogether too heterogeneous a class of stylistic effects, effects which range from "semantic tension" to "syntactic parallelism." Such a lack of internal discrimination detracts, I feel, from what nevertheless remains an extremely stimulating first pass over this infuriatingly elusive material.

My own employment of the term "aesthetic" will therefore be more narrowly restricted. In this study I shall use it to refer only to *those features located in the surface form of any work of art that are experienced by the reader as functions of time or space.* That aesthetic features exist only at the surface level divorces them, clearly, from much of the technical material discussed in chapter 2. That they exist as "functions of time or space" places them equally firmly outside the legitimate domain of interpretation—a point to which I shall return in due course. But a more distinct impression of what I do in fact intend by this definition may be gained from considering a third observation: that aesthetic features themselves exist independently of any one artistic medium, being applicable with equal success to music, the visual arts, or poetry.

Let us consider a couple of examples. At this particular level of abstraction a classical fugue may be said to instantiate musically the same aesthetic effect as the iterated visual pattern in a rug or on a ceramic tile. A similar correspondence relates the temporal syncopation of jazz rhythms in the musical sphere to the spatial and metrical off-lineation of Gwendolyn Brooks' "We Real Cool":[12]

> We real cool. We
> Left school. We
>
> Lurk late. We
> Strike straight. We . . .

This kind of broad aesthetic equivalence between different artistic media has of course been noted before, even by stylists, who are often poorly versed in aesthetic theory. Insufficient care has been devoted, however, to noting its scope, especially with respect to the verbal arts; as a result, a clear picture of its implications for literature has failed to emerge. Donald Davie, for example, cites approvingly a very suggestive remark from Susanne Langer's *Philosophy in a New Key:*

> [The] tension which music achieves through dissonance, and the reorientation in each new resolution to harmony, find their equivalents in the suspensions and periodic decisions of propositional sense in poetry.[13]

On the one hand, I too am happy to accept the broad correspondence that Langer is trying to establish here. But on the other, I cannot help regretting that her actual formulation of the equivalence effectively equates two very different kinds of phenomenon. "Suspension" assuredly belongs in any glossary of aesthetic terms, applicable alike to music and to verbal expression. It differs crucially from the cognate term "suspense"[14] precisely in its perceptual vividness and its relative lack of emotional connotations. We can effectively *perceive* something being suspended either in time (as with the arrival of a thunderclap) or in space (as with the arc of a half-built highway overpass). The term with which Langer links suspension in her discussion, however, does not describe an aesthetic phenomenon at all under my definition. "Tension" constitutes just one of several interpretive reactions that we might (or might not) in a given instance correlate with a suspended aesthetic structure. To compare the two is something of an apples-and-oranges exercise.

An aesthetic effect, then, is created by and in the surface features of a work of art. Its existence is not uniquely related to a particular artistic medium, nor should it be confused with the various interpretations that we may subsequently place upon it. Related by definition to a work's form rather than to its interpretation, aesthetic effects are indeed as devoid of *a priori* meaning as phrase-structure rules or the Tensed S Condition.

Naturally, such a narrow definition couched in such strong terms will entail all kinds of testable consequences for a theory of stylistic analysis that makes use of "aesthetic features" in this sense. Let us briefly review one of its more obvious predictions. Dryden's *technical means* of achieving the *aesthetic effect* of distance or delay in the passages studied early in this chapter were seen to differ radically from Byron's means of producing precisely the same effect in "Childish Recollections." My assertion that aesthetic effects are also meaning-independent now suggests in addition that the *interpretations* readers place on the delay that each poet creates might likewise differ. I do not wish here to preempt the business of chapter 4, where I shall discuss in detail the interpretations of stylistic choices. Still, it does seem to me that whereas Dryden seeks an effect of "emotional climax" in his ode, Byron rather contents himself in his couplet with a simple sense of "rhetorical finality." To the extent that I am correct in this assessment, my assertion that the level of aesthetic effects constitutes an entirely autonomous arena for syntactic manipulation receives preliminary support. For it is *only* at that one rather abstract level of analysis, we now see, that these two passages unmistakeably share any stylistic feature: their common reliance upon a strategy of delay.

Since aesthetic features are equally relevant to all kinds of art criticism, stylistics itself may benefit from a distinct term uniquely applicable to aesthetic judgments about *verbal* style. Wherever a particular aesthetic effect is realized in poetry using syntactic material, therefore, I shall apply the term *perceptual* to the statements that stylists use to describe that phenomenon. My remarks through-out the opening section of this chapter about the respective styles of Dryden and of Byron fall, of course, within this domain. In the re-maining pages of the chapter I shall offer a number of further exam-ples which will, I hope, clarify my theoretical assertions in the preceding paragraphs and at the same time give some hint of the variety and subtlety of readers' judgments in this area as a whole.

As the discussion thus far may already have revealed, I am my-self an enthusiastic amateur as an aesthetician. It seems to me how-ever that aesthetic effects as I have defined them fall into at least three classes:

(a) Features of *proportion* define our perception of what is *rela-tively* large or small, long or short within a given work. Syntactic distance or delay would thus represent a typical perceptual sty-listic effect taking its lead from a feature of aesthetic proportion.

(b) Aesthetic *scale* refers to the *overall* or *absolute* dimensions within which a work of art or its component parts are con-structed. As a mural demands an appreciation different in some respects from that appropriate to a miniature, so in poetry a couplet and an epic will be differently perceived. The need to characterize these distinct perceptions will result in stylists for-mulating specifically perceptual judgments about scale.

(c) *Pattern,* finally, is the aesthetic effect whose presence in literary texts has been most widely discussed and accepted by styl-ists in the past. (Indeed much of Cureton's dissatisfaction with stylistics as a discipline is due to what he sees as its almost obses-sive concern with this aspect of stylistic analysis—to the virtual exclusion, he claims, of sensitive interpretation.) This area may, then, be a good one from which to begin our exploration of perceptual stylistic analysis.

III

The stylistic literature is indeed long on books and articles that examine various poets' exploitation of abstract syntactic patterning in their works.[15] There remains nevertheless a great deal to be said about the many subtle variations that may be played on this simple theme and about the connections between perceptual patterning on the one hand and matters such as genre and period styles on the other. Let us begin by outlining the basic concepts involved.

Patterns of various sorts, I take it, form part of mankind's general aesthetic code. They are perhaps most easily recognized when instantiated as sequences of meaningless symbols such as letters of the alphabet. In this study, I shall rely on only three such pattern types: *chiastic* patterns (a b . . . b a), involving simple inversion of just two elements; *concentric* patterns [a b c (d) . . . (d) c b a], mirror-image sequences of more than two elements; and *parallel* patterns [a b c . . . a b c (. . . a b c)], repetitions of sequences of elements in uninverted order. Stylists who have done any work at all at what I am calling the perceptual level of analysis will immediately recognize these aesthetic patterns as the basis for arrangements of syntactic material that are common in literary texts, as in these rather straightforward cases:

> *Chiasmus*
> Watch all their Ways, and all their Actions guide:
> ("The Rape of the Lock": PAP, 225: 88)
>
> *Concentricity*
> As you meet it, the Land approacheth you.
> ("Astraea Redux": WJD I, 29: 253)
>
> *Parallelism*
> Squeezed in 'Fop's Alley,' jostled by the beaux,
> Teased with his hat, and trembling for his toes;
> ("Hints from Horace": BPW, 133: 311–312)

Naturally, such simple cases do not exhaust by any means the many configurations actually employed by poets, but they will provide a sufficient basis for making several useful preliminary observations.

It is no coincidence, for example, that I selected as my three paradigm citations lines from the works of two major Augustan poets, Pope and Dryden, and a couplet from a poem of Byron's which he referred to in his correspondence as "that Popean poem."[16] Syntactic patterning has long been recognized as a major stylistic trademark of the Augustan period of English poetry, and taught as such in English literature classes. But many pitfalls await the teacher who advances this generalization too incautiously, for equating patterned syntax too glibly with Augustan style may lead one to overlook a more *truly* characteristic feature of Augustan poetic syntax, as we shall see. So simple a rule of thumb may thus equip the student with an analytical tool that is in practice prone to serious malfunction.[17]

For a start, it takes no great effort to uncover examples of perceptual patterning in works that belong both chronologically and philosophically to the consciously anti-Augustan reaction of the early nineteenth century. As the first of two such examples, let us consider the style of one of Shelley's early works, *Queen Mab*. Seldom read except by Shelley scholars, *Queen Mab* suffers from a number of serious faults, not the least of which are its grandiose ambition and cosmic perspectives. Carlos Baker sums up the opinion of many critics when he describes this poem as "a distempered and unoriginal vision, mediocre as verse, and something less than mediocre as history."[18] It is also Baker, however, who seems almost to surprise himself when he notes of the "synthetic poem that results":

> Shelley does a better job with it than one would have supposed possible. . . . *By the use of . . . the device of surveying past, present, and future from a suprahistorical plane,* he achieves a certain unity.[19]

Shelley himself does nothing to conceal his dependence on the rather transparent expository ploy that Baker here applauds:

> . . . Spirit, come!
> This is thine high reward:—the past shall rise;
> Thou shalt behold the present; I will teach
>   The secrets of the future.
> (CWS I, 77: 64–67)

But other poets have structured narrative works along similar lines without letting that choice affect their stylistic behavior (Dryden's "The Hind and the Panther" is such a poem, as Earl Miner argues[20]). I suspect, therefore, that Baker has happened upon a factor of more than trivial importance when he draws attention to triple-ness as a source of unity in *Queen Mab*. Triadic structure, I suggest, offers Shelley in this poem an organizing principle that supplies, not only narratively but at various levels in the text, the coherence that his philosophical and historical material would otherwise totally lack.

Triads (parallel perceptual patterns, in the terminology of this chapter, with exactly three repetitions of the syntactic sequences involved) certainly occur at every syntactic level within this poem.

Almost every verse paragraph, for example, yields at least one phrase composed of three conjoined members of the same lexical category, many of these combinations being bolstered by alliteration to counter their natural tendency to slip into weak tautology:

> lovely, wild and grand (CWS I, 69: 70)
> astonishes, enraptures, elevates (CWS I, 69: 71)
> Rots, perishes, and passes (CWS I, 71: 156)
> passions, prejudices, interests (CWS I, 78: 103)
> Strangers, and ships, and merchandize (CWS I, 81: 201)
> morals, law and custom (CWS I, 94: 130)
> quake, believe, and cringe (CWS I, 96: 219)
> judgment, hope, or love (CWS I, 97: 256)
> frozen, unimpassioned, spiritless (CWS I, 98: 25)
> weak, unstable and precarious (CWS I, 118: 206)

Nor can Shelley's reliance on lexical triads of this kind be dismissed out of hand as a compulsive structural "twitch," since there is, at least sometimes, method to this apparently scatter-fire technique. Both T. S. Eliot and Melvin T. Solve have noted the general importance of "catchwords" in *Queen Mab*,[21] recurrent words and phrases associated with both the virtues Shelley sought to recommend to his readers and the vices he so vigorously condemned. Neither critic comments, though, on the distinct likelihood that these catchwords will turn up in those persistent (and again sometimes alliterating) triadic constructions:

> *Virtues*
> youth, integrity, and loveliness (CWS I, 98: 14)
> peaceful, and serene, and self-enshrined (CWS I, 120: 256)
> Love, freedom, health (CWS I, 121: 15)
> virtue, love, and pleasure (CWS I, 129: 75)
>
> *Vices*
> kings, and priests, and statesmen (CWS I, 92: 80)
> Kings, priests, and statesmen (CWS I, 93: 104)
> priest, conqueror, or prince (CWS I, 97: 237)
> Ruin, and death, and woe (CWS I, 92: 85)
> ruin, vice, and slavery (CWS I, 93: 99)
> The ruin, the disgrace, the woe of war (CWS I, 99: 68)

As these and many other similar examples show, Shelley's employment of triadic series often correlates with and accentuates major oppositions he wished particularly to pinpoint for discussion in

Queen Mab. At the very least, the discovery of this correlation between syntactic patterning and thematic emphases invites us to
study a good deal more closely a stylistic feature that at first seemed
trivially mechanical.

Shelley's preference for syntactic triads is no less evident if we
shift our focus from the level of lexical categories to that of phrasal
and clausal constructions; triple parallel patterns continue to leap
from every page:

So bright, so fair, so wild a shape (CWS I, 69: 74)

all virtue, all delight, all love (CWS I, 98: 19)

Blighting all prospect but of selfish gain,
Withering all passion but of slavish fear,
Extinguishing all free and generous love
Of enterprize and daring, . . .
(CWS I, 100: 84–87)

This commerce of sincerest virtue needs
No mediative signs of selfishness,
No jealous intercourse of wretched gain,
No balancings of prudence, cold and long;
(CWS I, 104: 231–234)

The larger the syntactic units of which the triad is composed, of
course, the greater the opportunity to embellish the whole by varying details of the internal structure of individual members. At the
same time, the underlying perceptual reality remains the same in
each case, triadic parallelism running through the syntactic fabric of
Queen Mab as insistently as the beat of a Viennese waltz.

Perhaps the most beautiful and certainly the most complex example of syntactic patterning in this poem occurs, appropriately, at
one of the poem's several thematic turning points. For 213 lines at the
beginning of Section V, Shelley has ruthlessly attacked the coercive
power of "commerce," an aspect of "civilization" that he implausibly
blames for having caused virtually every evil known to man. At line
214, however, this ranting abruptly gives way to a calmer tone as the
poet prepares his readers to consider his own (highly idealistic) alternative goal for inspiring human actions, "[the] consciousness of good"
(line 223). It is this nine-line transitional passage to which we may

now turn our attention, noting first that it displays a particularly heavy density of "local" syntactic triads such as those exemplified in the preceding paragraphs.

A simple lexical triad in line 222, for instance, appears positively normal, given the bias in favor of such constructions throughout this poem:

> There is a nobler glory which . . .
> Imbues his lineaments with dauntlessness,
> Even when, from power's avenging hand, he takes
> Its *sweetest, last* and *noblest* title—death;
> (CWS I, 104: 214, 220–222; emphases mine)

Equally unsurprising, though slightly richer for its pleasing thesis-antithesis-synthesis sequence, is the placement of three finite verbs, one each in lines 214–216 of this passage:

> There is a nobler glory which *survives*
> Until our being *fades,* and, solacing
> All human care, *accompanies* its change;
> (CWS I, 104: 214–216; emphases again mine)

Shelley neatly captures in these verbs, first, the lifelong strength of our "nobler glory" wherever absolute good rather than pecuniary gain is our goal; second, his awareness of man's mortality; but also, third, his conviction that the passing of life will not necessarily entail the total loss of that glory, which may in some undefined way "accompany" our "change."

We may conclude our survey of relatively local triadic patterning in this pivotal passage by observing a slightly more complex arrangement of phrasal triplets in lines 217–219. I transcribe the lines themselves on the next page, and indicate in Figure 11 the particular parallel pattern that I have in mind.

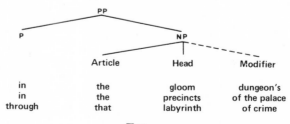

FIG. 11

There is a nobler glory which . . .
Deserts not virtue *in the dungeon's gloom,*
And, *in the precincts of the palace,* guides
Its footsteps *through that labyrinth of crime;*
(CWS I, 104: 214, 217–219; emphases my own)

(We may note in passing that this syntactic parallelism is again more than merely decorative. The word *palace* here finds itself in distinctly unsavory company, *dungeon* and *crime* being the corresponding modifiers in the flanking NPs. Such an association, of course, is perfectly in tune with the general derogation of traditional power structures that forms the major topic of this poem.)

All of the observations that we have made so far about parallel triadic patterning in this important transitional section of *Queen Mab* pale, however, when one steps back sufficiently far to view the nine-line passage as a whole:

There is a nobler glory which [S1 survives
Until our being fades, and, solacing
All human care, accompanies its change;]

[S2 Deserts not virtue in the dungeon's gloom,
And, in the precincts of the palace, guides
Its footsteps through that labyrinth of crime;]

[S3 Imbues his lineaments with dauntlessness,
Even when, from power's avenging hand, he takes
Its sweetest, last and noblest title—death;]

We have already seen that each of the major clauses constituting this passage (S1, S2, and S3 as indicated above) contains its own *internal* triadic pattern. Now, however, from a higher vantage point, we can isolate three further correspondences linking, *externally,* their respective sentential structures:

(a) each matrix clause consists of two smaller clauses linked by a conjunction;
(b) the second clause in each case contains fronted (prepositional or participial) material; and
(c) the second clause in each case also contains in its object NP an anaphoric pronoun *(its)* which refers to a thematically prominent NP in the first part of the construction.

The complete pattern is perhaps best appreciated when the structures of the three clauses are simplified so as to permit close comparison, as in Figure 12.

In all, therefore, we find in this important passage from Section V of *Queen Mab three three-line* constructions whose internal syntactic structures embody *three independent triadic* parallelisms, but which also *share* the *three* significant structural features defined in points (a) through (c) above.

Viewed dispassionately, Shelley's valiant attempt in *Queen Mab* to persuade his readers of the attainability of a world governed only by people's pursuit of abstract good seems doomed to failure from the very beginning. Could man operate at all, we find ourselves asking, if deprived of all the major traditional motives for success, "gold," "sordid fame," and even "hope of heavenly bliss" (another triad!)? It is this extreme naivete, certainly, that has led critics to reject out of hand any *philosophical* claim to fame for the poem. Yet, as we saw at the beginning of this discussion, critics do grudgingly acknowledge some *poetic* merit in *Queen Mab*. Our perceptual analysis of Shelley's style demonstrates, I think, how this may be. For it is in the rhetorical force of his perceptual style that Shelley comes closest to convincing us that his vision may have some chance of success, however slight. Only the relentless pressure of his hierarchically ranged triads, that is, shows any sign of carrying the day (it too, of course, falling short as soon as we recognize the enormity of the

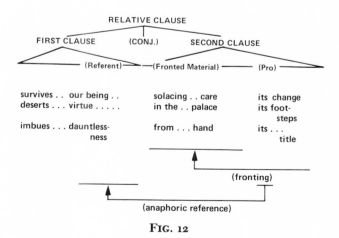

FIG. 12

issues to which Shelley is seeking our essentially irrational, emotional assent).[22]

I have examined at some length the role of syntactic patterning in *Queen Mab* partly, to be sure, because I have not yet found any reference to that feature of this particular poem's style in standard critical commentaries. I shall also have more to say in due course about what its presence implies for our conception of Augustan and Romantic syntactic styles. Let us first, however, devote a little more space to considering certain consequences of these perceptual patterns themselves. In particular, let us examine the way in which such patterns may predispose readers toward certain interpretations of quasiambiguous syntactic structures even where those interpretations involve a certain amount of deviance from standard analytical procedures.

The same section of *Queen Mab* that furnished us with so much material for analysis in the preceding paragraphs—Section V—also includes the lines:

          . . . gold:
Before whose image bow the vulgar great,
The vainly rich, the miserable proud,
The mob of peasants, nobles, priests, and kings,
(CWS I, 99: 55–58)

Shelley's catalog of those who "bow" to commerce's "all-enslaving power" ranges widely; a technical analysis would take note of seven independent NPs. The task of assigning an internal structure to the larger NP that dominates them and constitutes the ultimate subject of "bow" would still be a simple one, however, under normal circumstances. The overt presence of an interpretively crucial conjunction *(and)* between the two rightmost conjuncts (". . . priests *and* kings") would dictate that, as in the (a) structure of the figures that follow, all seven coordinate NPs be accorded coequal status, since the syntax of standard English provides that conjunctions between coordinated constituents of equal rank *other than the rightmost such conjunction* may be, and usually will be, deleted. This technically unremarkable conclusion runs into trouble only because structure (a), shown in Figure 13, at least by my reckoning, fails to represent readers' most likely interpretation of this passage. In what follows, I shall show that our awareness of Shelley's characteristic employment of perceptual

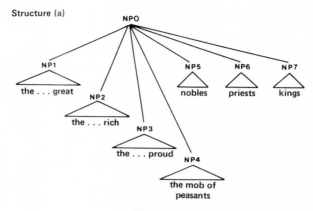

FIG. 13

patterning throughout this poem probably influences us to reject
structure (a) and to accept instead a somewhat deviant syntactic
analysis.

The first three NPs of the seven specified by Shelley for censure
clearly form a triad, linked by the congruence of their internal syntactic structure in a manner now thoroughly familiar to us and illustrated in the structure (b), shown in Figure 14. Let us hypothesize,
then, that the reader relies on his perception of this parallelism to
assign these three NPs to a single node within the dominating phrase.
Such an assumption gives us in turn structure (c), shown in Figure 15,
to represent his overall analysis of these lines.

Even that structure, however, fails to reflect what I see as the
most probable interpretation of this passage. The three nouns *nobles,
priests* and *kings* belong, after all, to one of those classes of "catchwords" that Shelley employs so often as a special code in this poem
(see note 21 and the examples to which that note is appended). The
noun *peasants,* by contrast, certainly does not fall into that category.
Thus the reader finally opts, I think, for yet another parsing, as
illustrated in structure (d), shown in Figure 16. Significantly, hypothe-
sizing triadic internal structure for both NPA and NPB in this analysis
also creates an *additional* triple division within the highest phrase,
NPO, thus compounding the already rich hierarchy of triads that
makes up this construction.

Let us be quite clear about what is involved in the reanalysis that

Structure (b)

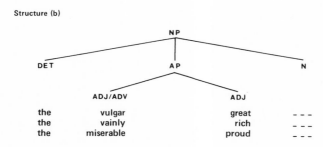

Structure (c) .

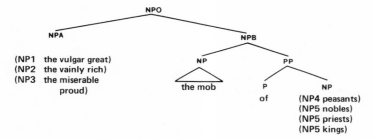

FIG. 14 and FIG. 15

Structure (d) .

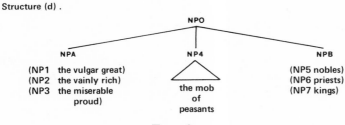

FIG. 16

I am proposing here. In an everyday context, Shelley's sentence as written could be assigned *only* structure (a) of the three described, since standard syntactic practice would require in the other two cases inclusion of additional conjunctions to assist readers in identifying their respective more complex structural configurations:

for structure (c): the vulgar great, the vainly rich, *and* the miserable proud, *and* the mob of peasants, nobles, priests, and kings.

for structure (d): the vulgar great, the vainly rich, *and* the miserable proud, the mob of peasants, *and* nobles, priests, and kings.

In assigning to Shelley's words the structure shown in (d), then, the reader is not just choosing one of a number of competing structural analyses. He is positively rejecting the most straightforward available analysis in favor of another that is at least mildly deviant in its omission of structurally decisive coordinating conjunctions. His initial willingness to entertain this possibility depends, I take it, on a perceptually induced predisposition to seek out syntactic triads wherever possible in this particular text. Application of such a general heuristic strategy to these specific lines then receives support from other features of the poetry [in the form of the syntactic parallelisms between NPs 1, 2, and 3; in the semantic relatedness of NPs 5, 6, and 7; and finally also in the "triple triad" structure that emerges from the (d) structure].

A stylist who argues along these or similar lines risks being misunderstood on several counts. His readers may assume, first, that he proposes to base his *technical* account of a given passage on *perceptual* features in its immediate context. This is certainly not the case. Technical analysis deals with matters of linguistic competence, strictly interpreted. If readers assign structure (d) to Shelley's lines from *Queen Mab* as I have suggested, then they do so in outright defiance of their standard linguistic competence, a fact which it is the business of the stylist to make perfectly clear. By other detractors, the stylist may be accused of allowing his own pattern-seeking predilections to dictate structural subtleties that real readers could not, or at least do not, appreciate. This is an altogether more complicated challenge, which we shall have to consider in depth in later chapters. Certainly my openness here to the consideration of perceptual patterns and their consequences has enabled me to advance some intriguing empirical claims about real readers' behavior. It will take the assessment of a number of such predictions to refine our understanding of the many ways in which perceptual and technical features of style may interact and of how both may then influence reading strategies (if indeed they do so at all). But in any case, as I shall argue in detail in chapter 5, the outcome of such "applied" research projects will in no way affect the perceptual component of the theory of stylistics as such, since stylists' aims are critical rather than psychological, geared to evaluation by the criterion of insightfulness rather than empirical accuracy.

Last, and most dangerous of all, is the related accusation that analyses such as these cross my own firmly drawn demarcation line separating "perception" from "interpretation." Let us briefly reexamine, therefore, the way in which matters of interpretation were introduced into the preceding discussion. It is a fundamental belief of the theoretical linguist that native speakers base their interpretations of each sentence, to a large extent, on the structure that their syntactic competences assign to it. Transformational and even structuralist syntacticians have always depended heavily on eliciting native speakers' intuitive interpretations when attempting to verify the details of their syntactic analyses. This dependence has never been held, however, to entail the existence of an incestuous relationship between syntax and semantics in linguistic theory; each component of the grammar can be terminologically and methodologically autonomous even though the linguist may make crucial use of the simple, and indeed unavoidable, fact that natural languages exist as means for conveying human thoughts. My stylistic analysis of the three lines from *Queen Mab* in the preceding paragraphs analogously involved an attempt to construct for them a syntactic structure that would accurately describe the interpretations that readers do seem to place upon them. While the aim was absolutely to mirror those interpretations structurally, though, the argument itself was formal and at no point depended on nonperceptual terms, assumptions, or conclusions.

IV

As an example of intricate syntactic patterning in the work of an English early Romantic poet, the triadic parallelisms of *Queen Mab* are by no means unique. Unfortunately, considerations of space will prevent me from devoting all the attention I might have wished to the major role played by *concentric* perceptual patterns in the poetry of another major representative of the same school, Samuel Taylor Coleridge. To demonstrate in full just how typical of his general style such perceptual devices are would demand a textual survey of major proportions. The three passages that I shall have time to discuss have instead been selected principally as further illustrations of some of the theoretical stylistic claims advanced earlier in this chapter and as starting points for the development of additional, more detailed observations on certain aspects of perceptual stylistic analysis.

Coleridge's "Reflections on Having Left a Place of Retirement," a poem originally subtitled "A Poem which affects not to be Poetry," opens with a deceptively simple descriptive passage:[23]

> Low was our pretty Cot: our tallest Rose
> Peep'd at the chamber-window. We could hear
> At silent noon, and eve, and early morn,
> The Sea's faint murmur. In the open air
> Our Myrtles blossom'd; and across the porch
> Thick Jasmins twined: the little landscape round
> Was green and woody, . . .
> (CPW I, 106: 1–7)

Analysis of the surface structure of these lines reveals just five independent clauses, each set off with either a period or a colon, none with more than four major constituents, as illustrated in this chart:

S 1.	Low was our pretty Cot	ADJ COP NP
S 2.	Our tallest Rose . . . window.	NP V PP
S 3.	We could hear . . . murmur.	NP V PP NP
S 4.	In the open air . . . blossom'd and across the porch . . . twined	PP NP V
S 5.	The little landscape . . . woody	NP COP ADJ

Nor does transformational analysis reveal for any of these sentences a particularly noteworthy derivational history. PP-Fronting has applied twice, once to each conjunct of sentence 4; a related movement rule sometimes referred to as *Niching*[24] has moved the PP in sentence 3 to a position in front of the direct object (admittedly not usually a very acceptable location for such shifted material); and the transformation of *Copula Inversion* has exactly reversed the underlying NP-V-ADJ order of sentence 1. None of these processes, though, is uncommon in English, especially in poetry, and on technical evidence alone one might be inclined to accept at face value the claim to an "unaffected" poetic style implicit in Coleridge's original subtitle.[25]

A full perceptual analysis, however, reveals unsuspected subtleties in the apparent artlessness of this opening passage. The surface syntactic form of sentence 1, we note, neatly reverses that of sentence 5. Sentences 2 and 4 contain, respectively, clause-final and clause-initial locative PPs. Sentence 3, finally, places its (temporal) PP medially, devoting to it a whole line of verse. If we now concatenate these structures, therefore, there emerges a strikingly symmetrical syntactic form for the passage as a whole, as illustrated in Figure 17.

It would be extremely simple at this stage to attempt to draw a variety of exciting "conclusions" from the discovery of this patterning in Coleridge's poem. One is tempted, for example, to argue that the mere existence of this concentric mapping gives the lie to the implications of prosaicness and lack of artifice that may or may not have been intended by, but are often drawn from, Coleridge's use of the term "Conversation Poems" to describe this and other similar works. In a different vein, as I myself have argued at length elsewhere, one might allege that a proper understanding of the perceptual form dominating this passage can help the student of Coleridge's work to appreciate more fully the peculiar attraction that "dells" such as the one he describes here held for the poet at this point in his career; their natural symmetry, reflected in the contrived syntactic symmetry of the poetry, brought order, coherence, and "relation" to a world that, Coleridge felt sure, was rushing headlong toward disintegration.[26] Most intriguing of all, perhaps, since Coleridge is not a poet noted for his humor, our analysis of this passage opens up the possibility of a play on words in line 6. Here Coleridge rejects the standard adverbial form *around* in favor of the more poetic *round*. Is this scene, we wonder as a result, a "round" or rounded (or concentric) landscape, besides being of course the "little landscape around"? Actively to pursue any of these hares at this point, however, would be to play right into the hands of those skeptics who already doubt the ability of stylists to

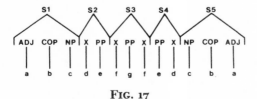

FIG. 17

conform to their own procedural guidelines. Such observations as those noted in this paragraph are, of course, primarily interpretive and hence out of place at this juncture. Having noted their promise as avenues for future exploration, therefore, let us instead focus rather more narrowly on the perceptual pattern that we have brought to light in "Reflections . . ." itself.

Given sufficient ingenuity on the part of the investigator, it is often alleged by both friends and foes of stylistics, at least one perceptual pattern—whether parallel, concentric, or chiastic—could be unearthed in the work of almost any poet.[27] Our response must probably be in the affirmative, but this suggests only that our next step should be to clarify, if we can, what exactly it is that makes some of those patterns worthy of notice, others mere "technicalities" within the perceptual field. Two factors, I suggest, may reasonably prompt the stylist to assume perceptual patterning in a given passage to be stylistically salient (although the patterning itself will, of course, be present whether or not it turns out to have very much importance in our overall stylistic analysis of the work in question). One such factor, the coincidence of syntactic patterning with some crucial aspect of an interpretation of the text—some such coincidence in fact as the ones I unsportingly alluded to and then abandoned in the preceding paragraph—will not be discussed in detail until we reach chapter 4. A second justification for according perceptual discoveries further consideration, however, and one that is equally relevant to our analysis of Coleridge's concentric patterning early in "Reflections . . .," turns out to be entirely proper even at this juncture in our deliberations: this is the fact that very similar perceptual patterns may occur in other compositions by the same poet. Where specific perceptual strategies *recur*, they become in essence legitimate topics for stylistic commentary by virtue of that simple fact alone.

The tricky task of devising dedicatory verses was not one at which the highly egocentric Coleridge excelled. "To the Rev. George Coleridge" is a deservedly little-read poem in this genre that combines exaggerated panegyric with bombastic but often self-pitying autobiography. Conspicuous, therefore, for their moderation and comparative emotional detachment are a few lines toward the end of the poem in which Coleridge recalls for his brother those moments when " 'tis to me an ever-new delight/To talk of thee and thine"

(CPW I, 175: 52–53). Among those moments Coleridge numbers, in particular, times

> . . . when, as now, on some delicious eve,
> We in our sweet sequester'd orchard-plot
> Sit on the tree crook'd earth-ward; whose old boughs,
> That hang above us in an arborous roof,
> Stirr'd by the faint gale of departing May,
> Send their loose blossoms slanting o'er our heads!
> (CPW I, 175: 56–61)

A simplified diagram of the surface syntactic structure of this lengthy clause, as shown in structure (a) of the two that follow, provides the basis for several statements about perceptual patterning as a feature of Coleridge's poetic style.

Structure (a) (Figure 18) differs from its most likely deep-structure source, structure (b) (Figure 19), primarily in that two PPs, *on some delicious eve* and *in our sweet sequester'd orchard-plot*, have been preposed, presumably by applications of PP-Fronting or the Niching transformation. In surface structure, as a result, the subject NP of S1 *(we)* occupies the pivotal position in a local concentric arrangement of like syntactic constituents, PPa-NP-PPb. This pattern, however, by no means exhausts the symmetries in this passage. S1, it will be noted, also contains a relative clause (S2) modifying its rightmost NP [*the tree (crook'd earth-ward) whose old boughs . . .*]. The NPe-S2-NPf substructure that effects this subordination may also, I propose, be considered as lying at the center of a symmetrical pattern. The syntactic evidence supporting my claim comes this time from the observation of a remarkable degree of congruence between the internal configurations of S1 and S2.[28] Consider these correspondences:

(a) both clauses are introduced by *wh-* words (*when* and *whose* respectively);

(b) the subject of each clause is separated from its verb by lengthy modifiers (by PPb in the first sentence; by both S3 and S4 in the second);

(c) two major modifiers are embedded preverbally in each sentence (PPa and PPb in S1; S3 and S4 in S2); and

(d) both clauses close with rather simple VPs whose final constituents are PPs (*on the tree* and *o'er our heads* respectively).

Structure (a) .

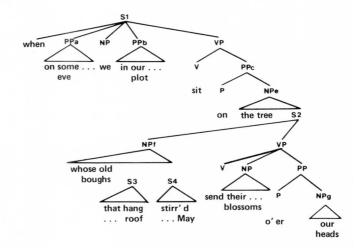

Structure (b) .

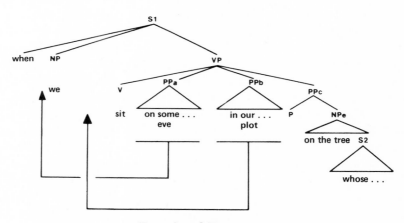

FIG. 18 and FIG. 19

S1 as a whole thus closely resembles S2; all that remains to reveal yet another concentric syntactic pattern is to imagine them balancing one another across the phrase *the tree whose boughs*. [While logic might perhaps dictate that the center of this pattern should be perceived to lie somewhere in the structural "space," so to speak, *between* the NPe and S2 nodes in structure (a), I suspect that readers are disposed to place such cruxes *at* nodes or *within* lexical items rather than between them. Hence my selection of *the tree . . . old boughs* as the core of this particular symmetry.]

The fact that this clausal concentric pattern appears so shortly after the phrasal PPa-NP-PPb symmetry at the beginning of the same construction (and indeed may be said properly to contain it) leads one in turn to consider the intriguing possibility that Coleridge is seeking to suggest by this perceptual device a relationship between the respective "foci" of the two patterns—the Coleridge family *(we)* and the old tree on which they sit. Although apparently speculative, this hypothesis receives support from the observation that exactly the same association of the tree with the family figures also emerges from a separate perceptual *parallelism* in this passage: that noted above as correspondence (d) between the prominent VP-final PPs of S1 and S2. My detection of such a delicate interaction between *a pair of concentric perceptual patterns* on the one hand and *a single parallel pattern* on the other should, I hope, satisfy even the strictest formalist. For those less puristic in their approach, however, I will include two further brief observations that stray a little outside the announced bailiwick for this chapter.

If we allow ourselves for a moment to take semantic as well as syntactic features into account as we develop and substantiate our analysis of this passage, then lines 57 and 61 of the poem will be found to define the *time* at which Coleridge's scene is set; lines 58 and 60, correspondingly, describe the *place* in which it is supposed to occur. As a result, we may use the lineation of this passage to demonstrate an additional A-B-C-B-A semantic symmetry. (At the center of this pattern, incidentally, there appear yet again the seated forms of Coleridge and his companions and the tree on which they rest.) My second ancillary observation concerns the relationship of the syntactic patterning in this passage to Coleridge's repeated use, sometimes even in nonpoetic contexts, of the metaphor of a tree to represent himself or his fortunes. In a 1798 letter, Coleridge wrote:

> I am like that Tree, which fronts me. . . . The beings who know how to sympathize with me are my foliage.[29]

Still more to the point, in an earlier passage from the very poem that we have been studying he exploits the same unusual comparison:

Some have preserv'd me from life's pelting ills;
But, *like a tree* with leaves of feeble stem,
If the clouds lasted, and a sudden breeze
Ruffled the boughs, *they* on my head at once
Dropped the collected shower; . . .
(CPW I, 174: 21–25; emphases mine)

Coleridge then goes on to identify brother George as the solid English oak amid the malevolent forest of the world:

. . . But, all praise to Him
Who gives us all things, . . .
Beneath the impervious covert of one oak,
I've rais'd a lowly shed, and know the names
Of Husband and of Father;
(CPW I, 174: 30–31, 33–35)

Looking ahead to the interpretive stage of the critical process, therefore, we might close the discussion of this passage from "To the Rev. George Coleridge" by suggesting that Coleridge's use of syntactic patterning to link to one another certain of its NPs constitutes an intriguing perceptual continuation and reinforcement of the "arboreal typology" introduced explicitly earlier in the text of the poem.

It would be foolish to conclude this section without making some comments on that most circular of all Coleridge's poems, "Kubla Khan." From the "stately pleasure-dome" itself to the "twice five miles" that Kubla "girdled round,"[30] and from the mystical invocation at the end of the poem to "Weave a circle round" the inspired poet back again to its striking, *phonologically* concentric first line, illustrated in Figure 20, every aspect of this amazing work contributes to a network of interlocking rings reminiscent of the famous Olympic emblem.

I have, however, offered elsewhere a fairly exhaustive stylistic analysis of this poem,[31] so I shall contribute here only one further

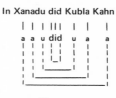

FIG. 20

brief example of the kind of patterning with which this chapter has been specifically concerned.

The final couplet of "Kubla Khan" reads:

For he on honey-dew hath fed,
And drunk the milk of Paradise.
(CPW I, 298: 53–54)

In the first of these lines, Coleridge creates the lexical compound *honey-dew,* though the modificational force of *honey-* might have been just as easily expressed as a postnominal *of-*prepositional-phrase (compare, for example, the compound *apple-juice* and its phrasal counterpart *juice of apples*).[32] At the same time he has also preposed the whole PP *on honey-dew* from its underlying postverbal position. Since the verbs *feed* and *drink* constitute a standard seman-tic collocation, we may use this fact, together with those just uncov-ered about the syntactic structure of line 53, to construct for the entire couplet a frame of a now very familiar kind as in Figure 21.

Simple syntactic symmetries of this sort are, I allege, Coleridge's stylistic "fingerprint"—a perceptually defined fingerprint as vivid, certainly, as those that Fish hopes to extract from technical analyses (see note 2 to this chapter). To recognize such perceptual fingerprints reliably the stylist will need to make himself adept in analysis of the kind developed throughout this chapter; in particular, he must be able to combine real syntactic precision with the less obviously lin-guistic skills of detecting and concatenating the subtle aesthetic pat-terns that are the raw materials for this kind of verbal artistry. But

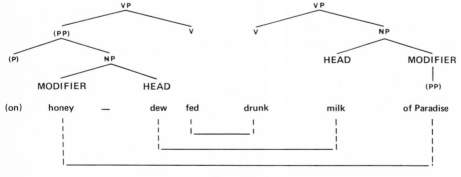

FIG. 21

not to invest in acquiring these skills and limit oneself strictly to technical remarks would be to miss the opportunity to pinpoint stylistic excellences such as those achieved by Coleridge in the passages that we have discussed, since theories of linguistic competence do not by definition embrace such concepts as structural concentricity or congruence.

V

Even stylistic studies that do take fully into account the existence of a perceptual dimension to syntactic form in poetry are not immune from serious distortions. The commonly accepted view, alluded to earlier in this chapter, that Augustan style is abnormally or even exclusively susceptible to analysis in terms of syntactic patterning is just such a case of mistaken emphasis (see note 17 and the associated discussion above). A variety of theoretical issues were addressed in the course of the preceding pages; taken together, however, they also develop what I take to be a strong case for believing that patterned syntax constitutes a powerful stylistic weapon in the expressive arsenal of at least two major *Romantic* poets. This being the case, any attempt to base a theory of how the styles of Augustan poets are "similar to" (and, *mutatis mutandis*, of how they "differ from") those of their successors in the nineteenth century on the mere presence of syntactic patterning in their poems is surely doomed to failure.

But what can then account for the way in which succeeding generations of critical scholars have fastened on patterning as *the* quintessential ingredient of characteristically Augustan verse? If patterning itself fails as a touchstone, where should we turn instead for a more adequate standard by which to identify this style which clearly *has* been felt by many accomplished readers to possess a distinct and discrete identity? In chapter 4, I shall argue that some discussion of favored interpretive strategies is indispensable to the formulation of a fully satisfactory answer to this question. We need not wait until then, however, to make significant improvements, at least, in our understanding of the differences between typically Augustan and Romantic *modes* of realizing perceptual patterns.

Let us begin by bringing the matter down to the level of specific cases. Early in this chapter, I quoted two lines from Byron's "Popean poem," "Hints from Horace":

> Squeezed in 'Fop's Alley,' jostled by the beaux,
> Teased with his hat, and trembling for his toes.

Shortly thereafter, I also discussed perceptual parallelism as a dominant feature of Shelley's style in *Queen Mab*. What, we now need to ask, distinguishes these two samples of syntactic parallelism, making one Augustan, the other neither more nor less patterned yet equally distinctively Romantic? Equivalently, we might ask what separates concentric patterning in line 253 of Dryden's "Astraea Redux" (also cited above),

> As you meet it, the Land approacheth you,

from the very same perceptual feature when it is repeatedly employed in Coleridge's poetry of the Romantic school.

Part of the answer lies, I believe, in the very special relationship established by Augustan poetic convention between perceptual *patterning* on the one hand and perceptual *scale* on the other. Statements about the aesthetic scale of a work, it will be recalled, define the dimensions within which each artist chooses to work his particular brand of creative magic—sonatina or concerto, summerhouse or cathedral. What is noticeable about perceptual patterns in Romantic poetry generally is that those dimensions appear to be very much a matter for individual choice. In this chapter alone, we have seen parallelisms and concentricities created by Romantic poets within the space of a few words (Shelley's lexical triads, for instance), within a line or two (the closing couplet of "Kubla Khan" is such a case), or over the course of an entire verse paragraph (as with the opening section of the conversation poem "Reflections . . ."). In many of those cases, the pattern has occupied a rather awkward fraction of a poetic line; in others, we have had to link half lines or even odd words with the lines preceding or following them in order to allow a given perceptual configuration to emerge. As a practical matter, in fact, it is altogether simpler to concentrate on *grammatical* units when examining a Romantic text for perceptual patterning than on conventional *poetic* units of whatever size or type; the orderliness implied by poetic structures such as the line, the couplet, or the stanza is as likely to obscure syntactic arrangements present in Romantic poetry as to reveal them.

The overall effect of Romantic perceptual patterning might usefully be compared to that created when a child builds a wall with a set of old-fashioned wooden building blocks. Each individual block may be right-angled, to be sure, but the considerable variety of their specific dimensions and colors makes for a final appearance of complexity and "irregularity." Where a pattern emerges from the child's construction, its parts may or may not correspond to individual blocks built into the fabric. In Augustan poems, by contrast, we find patterns far more akin to the "regular" brickwork of a Victorian building, since the sizes of the stylistic building blocks available to Augustan poets were strictly regulated by convention. The basic verse unit employed was set rigidly by metrical requirements at ten syllables, larger units almost always turning out to be even-number multiples of that basic structure because of the demands of the simple couplet rhyme-scheme. At the same time, poetic convention further dictated for the Augustan poet that these basic verse units provide a perfectly fitted frame for any stylistic effects he might also wish to introduce. It thus becomes a rather simple matter to isolate and describe perceptual patterns in such poems since their size and location relative to the poetic line have been predetermined by the poet's initial stylistic choice (or that of his "school"), a governing choice made initially in the subfield of perceptual scale.

Like all analogies, my comparison of the role of scale in poetic syntax to techniques for laying bricks will probably not survive close scrutiny. What I hope to have clarified by using it is that *the constant recurrence of syntactic patterns within segments of poetry of the same arbitrary length,* rather than their mere presence in the text, *is what makes them so prominent in Augustan verse.* [33] This theoretical claim of course has implications for an area far broader than the specific problem that suggested it here. My general conclusion should transfer rather smoothly, in fact, to cases in which the "segment of poetry" involved is not the heroic couplet; a similarly recurrent perceptual pattern within each separate stanza of a ballad, for instance, or a pattern that appears repeatedly within the triplets of a poem in terza rima should, I predict, benefit from precisely similar perceptual prominence. It is only the extraordinary dominance of one particular closed form throughout more than a century of English poetry, in fact—the absolute dictatorship, so to speak, of the heroic couplet—that has led us to associate too simplistically the syntactic patterning that it highlights with the genre itself. Stylistic analysis can now do literary criticism a considerable service by once again dissociating features of pattern from features of scale. As a result, readers may be taught to see perceptual patterning as an integral feature of many, potentially extremely varied poetic styles —the Romantic, in particular, as much as the Augustan—and to view Augustan poetic syntax itself as adequately described in terms of perceptual patterning only if the analysis in question also includes details of the characteristic scale of those patterns. In poetry of periods and genres totally unrelated to Neoclassical heroic couplet satire, readers will continue to expect varying degrees of syntactic patterning; they will also, however, appreciate fully its somewhat less obvious and less conventional character. Such a revaluation, I feel, is sorely needed in scholarship, in our textbooks, and in the classroom instruction of new and naive readers.

VI

One section of Pope's tongue-in-cheek apologia for the fickle behavior of Belinda, his heroine in "The Rape of the Lock," catalogs the "varying Vanities" with which the *"Sylphs"* contrive to stock "the moving Toyshop" that is every young belle's heart (PAP, 221: 91–104). Pope describes a "giddy Circle,"

Where Wigs with Wigs, with Sword-knots Sword-knots strive,
Beaus banish Beaus, and Coaches Coaches drive.
(PAP, 221: 101–102)

Pope's choice of syntactic form here displays far *less* perceptual patterning than would have existed had he left the four clauses that constitute this couplet in their underlying forms. Metrical considerations aside, in fact, Pope could easily have used two neatly matched pairs of clauses, the first repeating the syntactic configuration NP-V-PP, the second employing parallel NP-V-NP structures:

Where wigs strive with wigs, sword-knots strive with sword-knots, beaus banish beaus, and coaches drive (out) coaches.

Instead, the attested surface form shows that he has allowed Gapping, PP-Fronting, and some such rule as Dillon's Verb Final to
eradicate almost all signs of parallelism from the surface structure of
his sentence.[34]

By adopting this ostensibly un-Augustan tactic, Pope succeeds in
achieving a stylistic effect of an altogether different kind. Perceptually, the surface structure that results (and perceptual effects are, it
will be recalled, surface structure related by definition) jumbles together nouns and prepositions in an unruly and confusing mess.
Instead of orderly NP-V-NP or NP-V-PP clauses, the reader is con-
fronted in line 101, for instance, with the thoroughly improbable
syntactic sequence NP-P-NP-P-NP-NP and may legitimately feel that
he is being openly challenged to uncover some halfway plausible
analysis. We will address the issue of why Pope chooses this particular
approach in just a moment.

But contrast this case first with two lines from Dryden's "Mac
Flecknoe," in which the "aged Prince" of *"Non-sense,"* Flecknoe,
"burst[s] out" in an absurd mock-panegyric to his heir-apparent,
Shadwell:

> Heavens bless my Son, from *Ireland* let him reign
> To farr *Barbadoes* on the Western main;
> (WJD II, 58: 139–140)

As Pope did in "The Rape of the Lock," Dryden here uses PP-
Fronting to distort the underlying word order of his clause's VP
[underlyingly *(let him) reign from Ireland to Barbadoes* . . .]. In this
case, however, the surface configuration that results separates from
one another constituents that had in deep structure been juxtaposed,
an effect precisely the reverse of the excessive compression wit-
nessed in the lines from Pope's poem.

As might be expected, neither of these great artists misses his
own interpretive mark in thus selecting contrasted perceptual strategies. Dryden certainly achieves his purpose—to emphasize (or to
have Flecknoe emphasize) the magnificent extent of the "Domin-
ion" that will be Shadwell's inheritance—just as effectively as Pope,
in "The Rape of the Lock," recreates syntactically the bewildering
"mystick Mazes" of court society. To appreciate fully the achievements of each poet in this area, though, it is clear that we shall first

need to be able to discriminate properly at the *perceptual* level itself between Dryden's stressing of syntactic *distance* as his major stylistic effect and Pope's reliance instead on close *proximity* between syntactic constituents in selecting his surface form.

With the mention of syntactic distance (and its opposite, so to speak, proximity) we return to the category of perceptual effects with which this chapter began—effects dependent on our sense of aesthetic *proportion*. The examples of stylistic delay in Dryden's Killigrew ode and Byron's "Childish Recollections" discussed then, after all, depended on precisely the same fundamental attributes of syntactic structure as the cases cited here from "The Rape of the Lock" and "Mac Flecknoe." All four passages exploit particularly the temporal and spatial aspects of the linguistic code. (It is, by the way, not clear to me that these are separate syntactic concepts. In practice, it is certainly clear that readers will tend to associate some examples of suspension with temporal perception, since they will be vividly aware of the actual delay caused in their processing of a long or involved sentence. Cases such as Dryden's separation of *"Ireland"* from *"Barbadoes,"* by contrast, will be related most easily to the spatial dimension, since the topic being addressed is itself geographical. These biases result, however, from features built into the *semantic* contexts of the passages concerned; *syntactically* speaking, such cases remain indistinguishable. In each, the relatively close or relatively remote structural placement of syntactically related material is what contributes primarily to the reader's perception of the passage as a whole.) No abstract, formal pattern results from these poets' syntactic choices (replacing like constituents with letters of the alphabet, for example, elicits no internal regularities suggestive of deliberate patterning). Neither the *extrinsic* size of the constructions involved, furthermore, nor the *absolute* distance between their component parts has any bearing on our appreciation of the style of any of the passages (as would be anticipated in cases dependent on perceptual scale). Rather, as all of these examples illustrate, the description of proportional effects, in stylistics as elsewhere, differs from other perceptual activities in that it demands the use of open-ended scales and depends on purely relativistic assessments of form.

That various combinations of proximity and distance may be (and have been) interwoven by poets to yield fascinatingly subtle syntactic fabrics has been beautifully illustrated by Cureton in chapter 4 of his dissertation. In general, I have little to add to his illuminating discussion. The pages that have intervened since my last mention of his work, though, do allow me now to clarify somewhat the few reservations I have with regard to his taxonomic principles. My own belief that spatial and temporal distance are syntactically indistinguishable, in particular, accounts for my rejection of his use of this dichotomy as a taxonomic prime. His classification obscures what I see as very important syntactic similarities between cases of what he calls (spatial) "inclusion" on the one hand, and cases of (temporal) "simultaneity" on the other.[35] Especially after my comments in previous sections of this chapter, it should also be simple to predict that I would be uneasy with Cureton's inclusion of categories with titles such as "symmetry" in a list of what are for the most part proportional stylistic effects. My own preferences are for a descriptive machinery that emphasizes the very different natures of perceptual effects based on aesthetic pattern and on aesthetic proportion respectively. Neither of these theoretical reservations, however, should be seen to detract at all from the variety, informativeness, and insightfulness of the material that Cureton has amassed. His textual examples suggest some of the richness that even a few variations on the simple theme of relative distance in surface syntactic form can in fact provide—variations for which Cureton finds terms such as "contiguity, inclusion, fusion, interruption" and "intrusion." To pile up further examples here would be to waste ink on a task already well done.

I shall conclude this chapter therefore with just a single example from my own work, an example which illustrates both the subtlety of the effects that can be achieved merely by manipulating syntactic proportion and the important role that those effects may play in establishing overall coherence in a passage. William Wordsworth's narrator in *The Ruined Cottage* finds himself, as the poem opens, at the edge of "a bare wide Common," and describes for the reader the landscape around him.[36] In the course of this description, he notes how

        . . . all the northern downs,
    In clearer air ascending, shewed far off
    Their surfaces with shadows dappled o'er

Of deep embattled clouds.
(TMH: 3–6)

The derivational history of this sentence must, I take it, look something like this:

Underlying word order:
. . . showed far off [NP their surfaces [S[VP dappled o'er [PP1 with shadows [PP2 of deep embattled clouds]]]]]

After PP-Fronting of PP1:
. . . showed far off [NP their surfaces [S[PP1 *with shadows* [PP2 *of deep embattled clouds*]] [VP dappled o'er]]]

After Extraposition-of-PP applied to PP2:[37]
. . . showed far off [NP their surfaces [S[PP1 with shadows] [VP dappled o'er] [PP2 *of deep embattled clouds*]]]

While it is, of course, with the surface structure of this sentence that we are primarily concerned for the purposes of perceptual analysis, a review of the full derivation clarifies one important consequence of Wordsworth's syntactic permutations for our perception of that surface form. Four major syntactic constituents have to be correctly located in an overall hierarchical structure if this sentence is to be adequately analyzed: the noun-phrase object (NP in the labeled bracketings of the derivation detailed above); its modifying verb-phrase (VP), which in this case represents the residue of a nonrestrictive relative clause (S); and two prepositional phrases, one (PP2) embedded within the other (PP1). The version of this sentence that Wordsworth actually included in *The Ruined Cottage* places those four crucial constituents not in the most derivationally transparent A-B-C-D order illustrated in the "Underlying word order" above, but in the disjoint sequence A-C-B-D. The result, it seems to me, is a charming syntactic metaphor for the dappled sunlight described by Wordsworth's narrator; the now separated and alternating PPs, in effect, mirror syntactically what Wordsworth later calls the "interposed" effects of light and shade on the "northern downs."[38]

I shall return in the next chapter to a fuller discussion of the *interpretive* success that Wordsworth scores by his use of this particular perceptual strategy. For the present I content myself (one last time) with the purely perceptual observation that it is the precisely handled separation and distinctive placement of syntactic material in this particular passage that provides its stylistic "edge," the respective distances between *several* syntactic constituents being carefully balanced to achieve a particularly pleasing alternation.

VII

This chapter has, I hope, started a number of hares. I have covered several examples under each of the three main subcategories of perceptual effects resulting from poets' deployment of syntactic forms: those related to *pattern,* those related to *scale,* and those related to *proportion.* Along the way, various related issues may have demanded attention for a while: the nature of Augustan poetic syntax, for instance, or the ways in which perceptual patterning may affect readers' parsings of complex structures. I close, however, with a simple reaffirmation of the claim that has lain, unspoken perhaps, behind all that has been said. However excellent, however linguistically advanced its technical methods, and however appealing its critical insights, stylistics will disregard at its peril the completely independent (and independently complex) role of aesthetics in the functioning of syntax as a medium for poetic expression. Stylists need desperately to develop both a vocabulary and a methodology adequate to the very considerable degree of sophistication of poets' achievements in this important area.

CHAPTER FOUR

The Task of
Interpretation

> There are many ways of catching a possum. In his
> function as an interpreter, the critic's first job is to
> discover which possum he should catch.
> —E. D. Hirsch, *Validity in Interpretation*.

I

As his father's ghost haunts the unlucky Hamlet, so the grisly
spectre of mechanistic interpretation clearly stalks through the wak-
ing nightmares of many contemporary critical theorists, who seek to
exorcise the demon by writing lengthy attacks on stylistic criticism.
As is often the case with such obsessions, the potential dangers that
these scholars point to represent wholly reasonable fears. I would
myself heartily agree that no lover of poetry should let pass unchal-
lenged any suggestion that the meaning of a poetic text might be
discoverable merely by plugging appropriate values into a differen-
tial equation of linguistic variables. Such eminent good sense, however, verges on irrational paranoia whenever these opponents of the
stylistic approach aver that the worst *has in fact already happened*
—that stylists are actively claiming for their method that it is some
kind of critical Rosetta Stone that can decipher for us, as if by magic,
the meanings encoded in any literary text.

Take, for example, Barbara Herrnstein Smith's long tirade
against the papers that appear in the first part of Roger Fowler's
anthology, *Style and Structure in Literature*. Each of those papers,
Smith asserts, develops a slightly different version of the same basic
theoretical "formula," which she summarizes as follows:

> [S]omething in a literary work that is . . . manifest or "surface," S, bears
> some relation, R, to something else that is . . . obscure . . . or "deep,"
> X; therefore, by analyzing S, one may discover X.[1]

As a basis for the sweeping indictment of stylistics that follows it, this characterization labors under at least one serious misunderstanding; it assumes the primary goal of all stylistic analyses to be the "discovery" of a text's "deep" meaning. In Smith's view, the stylist considers both the analysis of S and the determination of R merely intermediate steps on the path toward an altogether more important end, the revelation of the mysterious, till-then-concealed X. This subtly distorted view of stylistic criticism did not originate with Smith, however. As early as 1973, and primarily in reaction to some of Roman Jakobson's more extreme pronouncements, Stanley Fish had begun accusing stylists of responding primarily if not exclusively to "the promise of an automatic interpretive procedure."[2]

In the paragraphs that follow, I offer a radically different, and I think more accurate, perspective on the stylistic enterprise. Stylistic criticism, I suggest, directs the spotlight not at X, the meaning of a text under scrutiny, but at R, the term in Smith's formula that represents the relationship obtaining *between* S and X. What principally fascinates stylists, then, is the "how" rather than the "what" of poetic expression, the "maze" that Irene Fairley suggests lies "between the poem, its configurations of words and sentences, and the reader's interpretation."[3] This focus, which, I assert, characterizes the best recent work in stylistics, has been described by Jonathan Culler as "an important reversal of perspective" in critical method precisely because it "[assigns] a secondary place to the interpretation of individual texts."[4] Its importance for stylistic criticism has also been aggressively championed by scholars such as Donald Freeman, Geoffrey Leech and Michael Short, and Muffy Siegel.[5] The point still bears reiteration here, however, in view of the frequency with which its simple intent has been misunderstood or avoided by unsympathetic commentators.

Ironically, it is Smith herself who notices one rather telling indication of stylists' preoccupation with R in the very papers she attacks, though she fails to recognize its full significance. In the course of her discussion, she berates stylists for permitting "R, the relational term," to become "a word or phrase of exceptional vagueness. For example, S 'might suggest' $X \ldots S$ 'embraces' X."[6] Her remarks again echo those of Fish, who had complained bitterly about

> statements like this; the verbal patterns "reflect" the subject matter, are "congruent" with it, "express" it, "embody" it, "encode" it, and at one point even "enshrine" it.[7]

But neither critic acknowledges the most obvious implication of the plethora of descriptive terms that both so perceptively detect. The proliferation of theoretical terminology within a single component of any theoretical model surely betrays an area of major emphasis and growth for that theory. Stylists' persistent gropings for words adequate to describe the many relations they uncover between the linguistic forms and the general interpretations of literary texts do not, that is, constitute lapses into "exceptional vagueness"; on the contrary, they signal these authors' awareness of the wide variety of ways in which verbal form may affect meaning, and, simultaneously, their frustration at the lack of nonmetaphorical language with which to discriminate among them. The "relational term," seen as an object for study in itself rather than as a trivial preliminary to the act of deducing an interpretation, forms the very core of the stylistic approach to literature.

Fowler himself proposes just such an emphasis on the techniques by which poets capture meanings in words when he insists that

> there cannot be a 'linguistic criticism' in the naive sense . . . [of a] mechanical discovery procedure for poetic structure. . . . An urgent priority for contemporary stylistics is [instead] to determine . . . *how* . . . systems of literary knowledge are coded in the structure of language.[8]

And the same priorities inform E. L. Epstein's admirable attempt earlier in the same volume to develop a somewhat more specific and practical agenda for interpretive stylistics in his essay "The Self-Reflexive Artefact." In that discussion, Epstein specifies as his goal

> to observe the relationship or lack of relationship between the principles of selection and arrangement operating on the elements of form to see whether they are determined or not determined by the particular state of affairs conveyed by the lexical constellation chosen.[9]

One may, with Smith, regret Epstein's convoluted exposition in this passage, but his message at least is a simple one. He announces that his paper will aim to improve our working knowledge of *how* widely disparate, vastly complex human thoughts and emotions ("states of affairs") are actually *"realized* in linear and segmental form syntactically."[10] The method Epstein adopts is to refine and extend a relatively simple classification of such methods of "realization" contained in Donald Davie's brilliant essay, *Articulate Energy,* and then to relate the resulting taxonomy to what he considers a dominant trend in our methods of evaluating "Renaissance and post-Renaissance poetry from . . . Western Europe and America."[11] The resulting discussion I find stimulating, informative, and classically "stylistic"; yet it has little if anything to do with *the provision of explicit readings for particular texts,* a point that seems to escape Smith as she launches her attack on the theoretically far less crucial second half of Epstein's paper.

This chapter, then, will continue the important task, begun by Davie and Epstein, of characterizing and categorizing the wide variety of relations that may from time to time obtain between *technical* and *perceptual* aspects of poetic syntax, on the one hand, and the *meanings* of the poetic texts in which they occur, on the other. That I shall term all such relations "interpretive" should certainly not be taken to imply, however, that a text is *to be interpreted* by relying upon them. The interpretive subfield of stylistics within my theoretical model constitutes quite simply the domain within which linguistic and aesthetic statements about the text of some poem may be compared, contrasted, or otherwise correlated with critical assessments of its meaning. To put this point another way, the actual process of achieving for oneself a satisfactory interpretation of that text is wholly independent of, and will generally *precede* (theoretically if not practically), even the earliest stages of an interpretive stylistic discussion of its technique.

I am tempted at this point to move directly to the enumeration of specific interpretive strategies announced in the preceding paragraph. Were I to do so, however, it might wrongly be inferred that I naively believed that stylists *never* concerned themselves with what I just referred to as the "process of . . . interpretation" or with the particular readings that evolve from that process. Such is clearly not the case, and it is not hard to reconstruct the logic that allows stylists to associate "interpretive stylistics" as I have strictly defined it above with "interpretation" as it is widely understood by pre-Post-Structuralist critical theorists. "As stylistic theory gradually improves our comprehension of how verbal forms *habitually* correlate with literary meaning," that argument runs, "critics will be able to rely with increasing confidence on syntactic evidence as they formulate and defend their interpretive hypotheses."

Inevitably, this reasoning runs afoul of Fish, who positively derides the attempts of stylists such as J. P. Thorne to "match up grammatical structures with the effects they invariably produce."[12] Fish has, for once, read aright the general purpose of studies such as the one he is criticizing—to "match up" (or correlate) structures with effects rather than to unearth meanings by way of structural analysis. But this useful insight is marred when his old skepticism reasserts itself in a subtly new form. In the sternly inflexible adverb "invariably" that Fish interpolates into his paraphrase of Thorne's analytical goal, we may detect again the worrisome presence of a familiar gaunt and ghostly figure; Fish's ever-present fear of mechanistic interpretation, to be precise, has driven him to overreact once more to a menace that has never actually appeared in the flesh. From what he has read, Fish has inferred that stylists regard their own stylistic evidence as wholly irrefutable, as interpretive "money in the bank."[13] This inference (which specifically denies, of course, the spirit of the adverb *habitually* that I chose when formulating my own paraphrase of the stylist's manifesto above) I believe to be fundamentally erroneous. In the real world, it seems to me, most stylistic critics remain fully sensitive to the enormous complexity of the interpretive process. Many would probably agree with E. D. Hirsch, who argues that in its earliest stages, far from being linguistically or in any other important sense "invariable," the whole complex procedure cannot be reduced to any "systematic structure" at all, "because there is no way of compelling a right guess by means of rules and principles." Only much later, in fact, long after an intuitive reading of the text has *already* been developed by some indefinable heuristic strategy or group of strategies, does "the systematic side of interpretation begin," as the critic attempts to distinguish more valid individual interpretations from less valid ones.[14]

Within such a comparatively orthodox theory of literary criticism, stylists' attempts to rebut Fish's charge of mechanism should take the form of responses to questions of the following kind: What constitutes *bona fide* stylistic evidence in the second, "systematic" stage of the interpretive process (the stage which Hirsch calls "the job of validation")? And what weight is to be attached to that evidence (in particular, *does* stylistic evidence enjoy some kind of privileged, "invariant" status)? To what extent, in other words, is stylistic evidence vulnerable to overthrow in light of other, nonstylistic critical testimony?

In his introductory essay to *Style and Structure in Literature,*
Fowler considers precisely this issue when assessing how papers such
as Epstein's that rely on stylistic methods in pursuing critical goals
will be read by the general public. He finds it particularly praise-
worthy that "it is natural to argue with [that] paper according to the
normal canons of critical discourse."[15] The "significance of the literary phenomena noticed" in that and other such papers, Fowler suggests, will be compared *on equal terms* with insights gained using
more traditional critical methods, a basis for evaluation with which,
as a stylist himself, Fowler appears perfectly content. Elsewhere in
the same volume, Freeman offers a more detailed scenario, but one
wholly consistent with Fowler's egalitarian philosophy:

> [A]nalysis of a poet's . . . manipulations of . . . syntactic processes can lay
> bare the deep form of particular poems—the form controlling meta-
> phor, theme, tone, imagery, and diction.[16]

Where one "deep form" determines ("controls") such diverse features of a literary text as its syntax, tone, and imagery, Freeman
surely implies, analysis of any one "surface" feature stands as good
a chance of revealing that form as analysis of any other.

In ideal instances of course, as Freeman himself points out,
the stylist's conclusions will turn out to "parallel and reinforce" arguments based on the study of "other strategies of design—metaphor, rhetoric, even meter."[17] To these kinds of *internally* motivated arguments, furthermore, one might very well add
arguments whose bases lie *outside* the text (narrowly defined) in
its biographical, historical, or sociocultural background. But where
agreement and harmony are the ideals, occasional disputes and
discord are inevitable. In such cases, I would strongly contend, stylistic critics seek no preferential treatment, acknowledging that an
"invariant" relation between syntactic process or syntactic structure and literary interpretation is neither probable nor desirable.
They fully anticipate, in fact, that their critical hypotheses will sink
or swim as each fails or succeeds in the fundamental critical task of
correctly characterizing readers' informed responses to the work it
purports to explain.[18]

I do not believe, in summation, that most stylists would wish to
dispute the claim which Smith reiterates so insistently:

[A]lthough "the verbal structure" of the poem may *direct* one's experience and interpretation of it, that structure cannot "control," in the sense of unequivocally *determine,* either of them.[19]

But "unequivocal control" exaggerates stylists' views of the role of syntax in poetic expression just as unfairly as Fish's notion of "invariance." (Irene Fairley, to cite only one example, chooses instead the phrase "stimulates and guides" when she attempts to describe the subtle effects that a text's language has on its readers.[20]) In the end, therefore, it could be said to be almost irrelevant whether or not one agrees with Smith that *"a significant aspect* of meaning in the poem . . . is necessarily variable, irreducibly indeterminate"[21] so long as stylists actually lay claim only to explicating *other* parallel or perhaps intersecting "aspects" of that same overall "meaning."

Despite considerable provocation (based often on misreadings or careless readings of their work), stylists have generally succeeded quite well, I submit, in moderating their claims, alleging only that we must allow to the language of any work of literature a measure of influence on the way that it is interpreted—a simple creed that may be found expressed in the italicized sentences with which I opened chapter 1 of this study. Perhaps the preceding discussion and the examples that follow will do something to convince all parties to this dispute of the remarkably small extent to which committed stylists and supporters of Fish and Smith need actually disagree on this important issue.

One final remark. Given the delicately balanced set of methodological assumptions that I have now attributed to stylists, it may often be hard to determine by which of two complementary routes a given stylistic assessment of a literary text actually evolved—even for the analyst himself. Was it his initial achievement of a valid critical insight into poem X that provided one anchor, so to speak, for the interpretive stylistic judgment that he went on to make about it? Or did his detection of a familiar stylistic technique affecting the syntactic form of a passage prompt in its turn a particular reading of the lines in question? Such hermeneutic conundrums, though, are characteristic of the critical process in general and by no means unique to the stylistic approach.[22] We may never know which den produced the possum to whose capture we suddenly find ourselves committed (extending for a moment Hirsch's metaphor from the epigraph to this chapter); but the possum itself is no less substantial for that, and no less worthy a quarry for our hunt.

II

Having thus completed our obligatory detour to consider the complexities of the interpretive process, we may return at last to the central topic of this chapter, the cataloguing of *interpretive stylistic effects*, narrowly construed. As a first step, let us recognize that many of the technical and perceptual phenomena described in earlier chapters of this study can by all means feature in a text without having *any* clear effect on, or correspondence with, its overall interpretation. The importance of this simple observation to a fair evaluation of stylistic theory generally will justify, I think, the following detailed consideration of one particular case in point.

In chapter 2 of this study, we examined rather thoroughly Shelley's syntactically anarchic style in "Adonais." I shall want to return to that material again shortly. But the technical feats that Shelley performed in that work he had first learned several years earlier, for we find him invoking precisely the same strategies freely in *Laon and Cythna* (the poem later published, only very slightly revised, as *The Revolt of Islam*). I have developed elsewhere a rather lengthy technical analysis of these syntactic aberrations in *Laon and Cythna*.[23] At this point, therefore, I shall rely on only two rather brief analyses of particularly intriguing passages as *pro forma* support for my basic contention: that this work abounds in constraint-violating syntactic brain-teasers.

The first of my two illustrations represents a striking example, indeed a "textbook" case, of syntactic center-embedding, in which both an adverbial subordinate clause and the relative clause that it dominates are bracketed by lexical material that belongs to their respective matrix sentences:

> From that lone ruin, when the steed that panted
> Paused, might be heard the murmur of the motion
> Of waters,
> (CWS I, 334: 200–202)

The most deeply embedded clause in this construction, [S3 *that panted*], is properly contained within the intermediate clause, [S2 *when the steed . . . paused*]. S2 itself, however, appears between the bulk of the main sentence, [S1 *might be heard . . .*], and its preposed locative PP *(From that lone ruin)*.

These three lines thus closely resemble in all relevant respects some of the contorted passages from "Adonais" discussed at length in chapter 2. In their own poetic context, however, they hardly qualify as a major stylistic curiosity. The stanza that they introduce incorporates a variety of syntactic complexities convoluted enough to mask almost completely even the rather considerable problems caused by center-embedding:

> From that lone ruin, when the steed that panted
> Paused, might be heard the murmur of the motion
> Of waters, as in spots forever haunted
> By the choicest winds of Heaven, which are inchanted
> To music, by the wand of Solitude,
> That wizard wild, and the far tents implanted
> Upon the plain, be seen by those who stood
> Thence marking the dark shore of Ocean's curved flood.
> (CWS I, 334: 200–207)

How many readers, I wonder, succeed on the first or even the second reading in parsing this long-winded sentence? Its problems are both formal and pragmatic. When we first encounter the phrase *the far tents* (line 205), to consider just a single pragmatic stumblingblock, it betrays no feature that might help us to associate it with any construction then undergoing analysis. Any attempt, furthermore, to resolve this anomaly by assigning that phrase its correct role as the subject of a second main-clause conjunct [*the far tents . . . (might) be seen by those . . .*] is promptly thrown into question by the freakish appearance of a completely aberrant comma separating that noun-phrase from its (foreshortened) verb-phrase. Such *pragmatic* problems beset the reader repeatedly as he completes this stanza of the poem. It is important to realize, though, that the stage was set for this whole syntactic disaster by the *formally* constraint-violating center-embedded construction with which the stanza—and our discussion of its syntactic complexities—originally began.

Those of my friends whom I have in the past challenged to

paraphrase my second example of constraint-violating syntax from *Laon and Cythna* have for the most part had to resort to pencil and paper in order to establish a plausible analysis. The passage in question occurs at the close of the third canto of the poem, when the hero, Laon, is rescued from a nightmarish end by a mysterious hermit who rows him across a lake to safety:

> And the swift boat the little waves which bore,
> Were cut by its keen keel, tho' slantingly;
> (CWS I, 298: 300–301)

We must assume, I take it, that the underlying syntactic form of this sentence is as follows:

> [S1 [NP1 The little waves [S2 which bore [NP2 the swift boat]]] were cut by its keen keel].

Deriving the surface form actually attested in Shelley's poem from this structure will involve preposing NP2 *(the swift boat)* not merely to the left of the relative clause within which it originated (S2), but beyond that, to the left of the *head* of that clause, NP1 *(the little waves)*, as shown in Figure 22.

I outlined in the course of chapter 2 the syntactic problems that Shelley causes for his reader whenever he extracts syntactic material from within tensed clauses, particularly when, in addition, those tensed clauses contain overt complementizers such as *which*. Com-

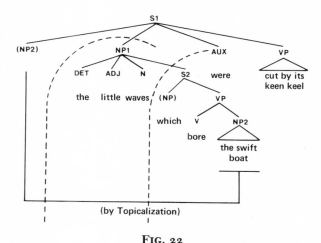

FIG. 22

plexity of both these kinds will inevitably be introduced by Shelley's inversions in the present passage, as a glance at the accompanying diagram clearly demonstrates. In this particular case, however, the awkwardness of the lines Shelley actually wrote is still further aggravated by the fact that the syntactic movement Shelley permits in the course of its derivation violates a *third* syntactic constraint, J. R. Ross's *Complex Noun-Phrase Constraint.*[24] This constraint, simply described, prohibits all movement out of clauses whose syntactic "heads" (their antecedents where relative clauses are concerned) are fully specified lexical items (rather than pronouns or syntactic "dummy" items). A glance back at the diagram that summarizes Shelley's derivation of his lines in *Laon and Cythna* demonstrates that such conditions are certainly met here, since NP2 is moved completely out of S2, a relative clause whose head is the lexical material, *the little waves.* Formally, therefore, the technical purist may arraign Shelley on no fewer than *three* separate counts as a perpetrator of syntactic disorders in this briefest of passages.

Ironically, it is Shelley's readers who must serve the concurrent sentences that he has earned as they battle to disentangle the syntactic puzzle he has created for them. Initially, after all, it is virtually impossible for readers *not* to misanalyze the surface structure they confront in these lines. They quite naturally take NP2 *(the . . . boat)* to be the subject of S1 and assume NP1 *(the . . . waves)* to have been generated originally within the embedded clause, S2. These perfectly reasonable assumptions yield a reading which we may paraphrase as follows:

The swift boat, which bore the little waves, were cut by its keen keel.

This represents, of course, an unacceptable reading because of the clauses' syntax (particularly the failure of subject-verb agreement) as well as their basic semantic uninterpretability. Yet correcting the misanalyses that such an approach involves will require of the same readers that they rely on their semantic intuition of what *must have been intended* to overcome strong prejudices against permitting constraint-violating movements in the course of syntactic derivations —prejudices which, as I have already noted in prior discussion, may be deeply rooted in the form and functioning of the human psyche.

Passages and constructions as complex as the two discussed in the preceding paragraphs abound in *Laon and Cythna*. One is tempted, indeed, to apply to this poem comments made about *Prometheus Unbound* by a reviewer for the infamous *Quarterly Review* who found Shelley's work "absolutely and intrinsically unintelligible," and singled out Shelley's syntax for particularly virulent attack, asserting that "both the ear and the understanding are disgusted, . . . by awkward and intricate construction of sentences." Nor is it at all difficult to find more recent critics who *have* in fact been at least this damning in their treatment of the style of *Laon and Cythna*. A. Clutton-Brock, for example, remarks of it:

> The poem is difficult to read as it is; in blank verse it would probably have been impossible.[25]

But the very feature of this poem's form that renders it least attractive to the general reader—the randomness and pervasiveness of the syntactic anarchies it contains—makes it a work of very great relevance and interest to our discussion in this chapter.

Laon and Cythna addresses a wide variety of issues—political, philosophical, religious, and social. A work much like *Queen Mab* in this respect, its attempts at comprehensiveness may again represent its most damaging flaw as a complete poetic achievement. Yet no one of its many themes, nor even a coherent grouping of some few among them, appears to conjure up in any consistent fashion the syntactically deviant language that I have characterized in the preceding pages. Beside Cythna and Laon themselves, this work also develops a large cast of characters—some named, others merely "a child" or "a Youth." Again, though, syntactic complexity is restricted to no one voice, at least so far as I have been able to discover. I can certainly conceive, then, of circumstances in which some technical or perceptual aspect of syntactic form, even in a poem as long and as involved as this one, might correspond productively with one of its thematic or narrative emphases. In actuality, I have been unable to detect any such correspondence in the case of *Laon and Cythna*. In discussing this work, I am repeatedly brought up short after completing my technical account of its style, frustrated in every attempt to offer interesting observations on the interpretive front.

(I do not, of course, view such a limitation as an embarrassment for the stylistic method of critical analysis. As I first suggested in chapter 1, the stylist's work may be carried on at any of the three analytical levels or by combining observations from any two or all of those levels. No analysis is fairly criticized merely for restricting itself to fewer than three levels. Nor, in principle, do I see any justification for valuing less highly works in which certain technical or perceptual stylistic features display no clear interpretive reflexes. I shall have more to say on this head at a later stage in this study; for now I simply observe that, in approaching works such as *Laon and Cythna,* the stylist may quite easily find himself with a great deal to say at one level of analysis—in this case the technical—yet be unable to take even the most preliminary steps toward an interpretive generalization.)

This situation contrasts vividly with that obtaining in the case of "Adonais." In that poem, a high concentration of constraint-violating structures in a single section of the text does at least invite the analyst to consider the possibility that syntactic complexity may be playing a determinate role in Shelley's composition. Selectivity, or what Geoffrey Leech and Michael Short would call "cohesion and consistency in preference,"[26] rather than mere virtuosity or carelessness, seems to be controlling Shelley's pen in the later of these two poems. Such selectivity merits our special attention, of course, because the additional detection of a principle capable of *explaining* the perceived distribution of syntactic effects would constitute our first serious candidate for consideration as an interpretive stylistic strategy.

The thematic structure of "Adonais" follows the sequence prescribed for elegiac poems by literary convention. In the opening stanzas, Shelley repeatedly stresses the irrevocability of death and in particular his personal sense of loss upon hearing of the passing of Adonais (Keats):

> I weep for ADONAIS—he is dead!
> (CWS II, 389: 1)

> Lost Echo sits amid the voiceless mountains, . . .
> And will no more reply to winds or fountains,
> Or amorous birds perched on the young green spray,
> (CWS II, 393: 127, 129–130)

> *He* will awake no more, oh, never more!
> (CWS II, 395: 190)

However, in the thirty-eighth stanza (and, appropriately enough, with the syntactically and semantically startling remark *"Not* let us

weep . . .") this elegy makes the anticipated turn towards reconcilia-
tion. In a sequence of images carefully chosen to match and to super-
sede those of the opening section of the poem, Shelley insists on the
enduring power of Keats' creative genius:

> Mourn *not* for Adonais.
> (CWS II, 401: 362; emphases in all three of these citations are my
>   own)

> He *is* made one with Nature: there *is* heard
> His *voice* in all her music, from the moan
> Of thunder, to the song of night's *sweet bird*
> (CWS II, 401: 370–372)

> He *hath awakened* . . .
> (CWS II, 400: 344)

From this reorientation stems, at last, the hopefulness and the calm
that mark the poem's perhaps rather unorthodox concluding question, "What Adonais is, why fear we to become?" (CWS II, 404: 459)
By the time we reach these closing lines, we realize that Shelley's
views have swung through 180 degrees, from an initial sense of cruel
deprivation and hopelessness at Keats' death to an imaginative recreation of a joyful reunion with his fellow artist, a reunion conceivable
only beyond the frustrations and restrictions of mortal existence.

Within this thematic framework, the violations of syntactic constraints discussed in chapter 2 of this study occur in only three, and
indeed in three *consecutive,* stanzas of the poem—Stanzas IV, V, and
VI. Nowhere else, despite repeated rereadings of the text, have I
been able to isolate a single phrase or clause whose syntactic structure even approaches in complexity the contortedness of these three
closely adjacent passages. In stylistic analysis, as indeed in any other
critical pursuit, a textual feature thrown into such dramatic relief by
its localized distribution within the work as a whole surely demands
our careful attention.

Stanzas IV–VI of "Adonais" contribute to the pessimistic early
section of that poem a brief historical survey of injustices perpetrated
on poets by their sadly unappreciative publics. Stanza IV specifically
laments the miserable fate of John Milton, who died "Blind, old, and
lonely"; Stanza V describes the failure of later poets' public reputa-
tions to reflect their individual merits ("*tapers* yet burn through that
night of time/In which *suns* perished"—my emphases); and Stanza

VI focuses on what Shelley sees as just one more example of such injustice, Keats' own unfair treatment as "the loveliest and the last" of the lyricists in Milton's line.

Those familiar with Shelley's other writings will recognize in the human imperfection that he laments in these stanzas a typical symptom of the postlapsarian world described at greater length in *A Defence of Poetry*. That world is one in which, Shelley claims, we mortals simply cannot shake off "the curse which binds us to be subjected to the accident of surrounding impressions" (CWS VII, 137). In the early stanzas of "Adonais," then, we witness at first hand this world untransmuted by poetic vision, where Shelley, as a representative of humankind, flounders about, unable to see recent events in their proper context or from a sufficiently elevated perspective. And it is in his attempt to convey this particular rather obscure state of affairs poetically, in his anxiety to capture the inadequacy of this all too "familiar world" which, as he says in the *Defence*, "is a chaos," that Shelley relies on a syntactic form that is also "a chaos," full of complexities and convolutions. At this point, early in the poem, as Shelley deliberately places himself on a par with those whose outlook he will later criticize, the wrong-headedness of the mundane standards by which he at first assesses and mourns Keats' death is suggested obliquely for the reader by the contortedness of the grammatical means by which he expresses his sorrow and anger.

But two forces, Shelley believed, were constantly working to ameliorate Man's sorry plight: history and poetry. The contemporary poet, aided by both his position in historical time and his aesthetic sense, represented all that was most promising for the future:

> It is impossible to read the compositions of the most celebrated writers of the present day without being startled with the electric life which burns within their words (*A Defence of Poetry*, CWS VII, 140).

It is, of course, this enduring "life" that Shelley celebrates later in "Adonais," poetic inspiration as a power that reveals once and for all the limitedness of a vision not mediated in this way:

> 'Tis we, who lost in stormy visions, keep
> With phantoms an unprofitable strife,
> And in mad trance strike with our spirit's knife
> Invulnerable nothings.
> (CWS II, 400: 345–348)

Yet how was Shelley to suggest for his readers, mere mortals and thus inevitably unfamiliar with this poetic super-vision, the character of that amazing higher plane of knowledge? For the clearer, purer, truer vision that great poets such as Keats could alone achieve, Shelley offers, if you like, the syntactic metaphor of a style clear of technical challenge and complexity. Toward the end of the poem his voice rings out boldly in simple clauses:

> The soft sky smiles,—the low wind whispers near:
> 'Tis Adonais calls! oh, hasten thither,
> No more let life divide what Death can join together.
> (CWS II, 404: 475–477)

This, I would claim, is Shelley's true "voice of poetry," a syntax as clean and uncluttered but also as "burning" as the "electric life" that he so much admired in the work of his contemporaries.

If we accept it at all, then, we accept Shelley's tone of calm in the closing lines of this elegy largely because his use of the English language has, throughout the poem, reflected and reinforced the contrast between the worldly and poetic visions on which his whole philosophy is predicated. An understanding of the crucial roles that syntactic complexity and simplicity play at different moments in this poem is thus at least as useful a critical tool as, say, a thorough historical knowledge of the relationship between Shelley's poetry and the *Defence*. Neither kind of information will, of course, guarantee us a more rapid or an absolutely "valid" interpretation of "Adonais." Both, however, do afford us the chance of a valuable insight into the philosophical assumptions that motivate Shelley's resigned, if not almost suicidal, tone at the end of this extremely challenging poem.

III

This chapter opened, somewhat combatively, with a defense of the stylist's right to seek out and to examine correlations between syntactic forms on the one hand and interpretive emphases or contrasts on the other. I immediately conceded that the potential for discovering such a correlation necessarily implied also the possibility that in certain cases no correlation would in fact present itself. Shelley's *Laon and Cythna*, or more precisely the pervasive and apparently undirected syntactic complexities in that poem, were adduced as an excellent case in point. Yet now we see that "Adonais," a poem by the very same author exhibiting certain very similar syntactic properties, belongs in an altogether different category so far as interpretive stylistic analysis is concerned. In this second poem, we can assign to each of the poles of one of the poem's major thematic contrasts an intuitively apt mode of syntactic expression. Passages describing mortal man's imperfect vision appear in a syntactic form that confuses the reader by flouting linguistic conventions. For sections of the poem intended to delineate the clearer perspectives of poetic vision, however, Shelley adopts a comparatively lucid, less baffling set of syntactic structures.[27] This correlation is one of those positive correspondences between syntax and interpretation that I earlier defined as the proper subject matter of interpretive stylistics. It therefore remains to assign that particular *kind* of correspondence a suitable name, if only for the sake of convenience, and then to establish more precisely the characteristics that qualify a given interpretive strategy for membership in that subclassification.

In selecting the term *mimesis* for such interpretive effects as Shelley's use of syntactic complexity in "Adonais," I am aware that I run a considerable risk of inviting controversy. I cannot help agreeing with Smith when she objects strongly to stylists' excessive reliance on the words *mime, mimetic,* and *mimesis.*[28] But of the few other terms that spring to mind from the literature, *icon, iconic,* and *iconicity* suffer from almost equal overuse and abuse. In any case, I shall shortly need to invoke that particular trio to name a second category of interpretive effects—effects that I shall want expressly to *distinguish* from those observed in "Adonais." By the same token, the notion of a *metaphor,* while useful metaphorically, remains notoriously imprecise and poorly understood wherever it is applied. I shall continue, therefore, to rely on the familiar *mimesis,* offsetting its decidedly checkered history by providing as full a characterization as I can of the term within the theoretical framework that I am developing. The same arguments, *mutatis mutandis,* will also have to justify my decision to employ the term *iconicity* for other examples that fill the coming pages. Neither this parallelism, though, nor the fact that I have little choice but to define each term by comparing it with the other, seriously undermines, I believe, the value of both as critical concepts.

The crucial distinction between what I intend by syntactic *mimesis* and what I intend by syntactic *iconicity* in the interpretive analysis of poetic style is best captured, I think, in the following pair of wholly artificial sample sentences:

> (1) Behind the door, ill at ease, I stood, expecting at any moment to betray my presence, and awaited his return. (MIMESIS)

> (2) Behind the door stood a tall man, and behind him, a little girl with bright red hair. (ICONICITY)

In the first of these sentences, we focus our attention on the speaker, and specifically on his mood and his predicament. The surface syntactic structure of the sentence helps to identify that predicament as one full of danger, the speaker's mood as one of nervous apprehension. PP-Fronting and other syntactic movement processes combine to create a general impression of disjointedness, uncertainty, and tentativeness—an impression that becomes immediately evident if sentence (1) is contrasted with its more standard paraphrase, (1′).

> (1′) I stood and awaited his return behind the door, ill at ease, expecting to betray my presence at any moment.

It is my contention that stylists should reserve the term *mimesis* for just such cases as this, cases in which it is an *abstract theme* of the passage under consideration with which syntactic features are being alleged to correlate. Our recently completed discussion of syntactic form in "Adonais" constitutes an excellent example taken from a major literary work, since there the abstract concept of flawed human perception provided a thematic correlate for syntactic complexity.

Compare with such cases sentence (2) from the preceding paragraph. Fronting the PPs *behind the door* and *behind him* in this construction achieves no dramatic mirroring of any thematic concern of its author. Instead, syntactic movement has here resulted in a surface structure in which the noun-phrase *the door* occurs, quite literally, as the first item that we encounter as we read through the sentence. The phrase *a tall man,* in deep structure the sentence-initial subject NP, thus appears "behind" the phrase *the door,* and the words describing the little girl only "after" that. In this sense, the physical (temporal and spatial) order in which the reader naturally processes these crucial referential NPs precisely matches the physi-

cal (spatial) relations that are claimed to hold within the scene described. To see how helpful such an interpretive aid from the syntax
may be, one need only contrast sentence (2) with its denotatively
parallel but untransformed counterpart, (2').

(2') A tall man stood behind the door, and a little girl with bright red
hair (stood) behind him.

Here the reader must envision the whole scene on the basis of the
sentence's semantic content; no clues from the syntax will help him
to "set the stage."

Where, as in sentence (2), a correspondence between syntactic
form and interpretation is based on *physical* rather than thematic
imitation, I shall use the term *iconicity* in referring to it. One need
not look far for examples of such iconic strategies, since cases of this
kind have long figured prominently in the stylistic literature; chapter
4 of Richard Cureton's dissertation, for a start, contains a challeng-
ingly full inventory culled from the works of E. E. Cummings ("high
priest," perhaps, of iconic syntax).[29] For those who do not wish to
move even that far afield in search of appropriate examples from the
works of major poets, chapter 3 of this study itself provided several,
though at the time we were focusing almost entirely on those examples' perceptual, rather than interpretive, analysis. Among other
passages discussed there, for instance, was one from Coleridge's "Reflections on Having Left a Place of Retirement." As a brief review of
that discussion will confirm, the striking concentricity that characterizes the syntactic form of the opening lines of that poem was held to
represent a perfect spatial icon for the concave valley, the "little
landscape round," that Coleridge sought to describe. In discussing
Wordsworth's *The Ruined Cottage* later in the same chapter, I
pointed out in a similar vein that the "interleaving" of structurally
related syntactic elements at surface structure in the opening lines
of that work resulted in an iconic recreation of the "dappled" sunlight that the poem's narrator studies and describes so carefully. And,
still in chapter 3 of this study, I pointed to one other, non-Romantic
example of syntactic iconicity, a simple line of Dryden's cited originally for its instantiation of concentric perceptual patterning:

As you meet it, the Land approacheth you.
("Astraea Redux": WJD I, 29: 253)

From our current perspective, this line represents a perfect icon in miniature—not, it is true, of the advancing king's *actual* progress, but of the reciprocal movement of both monarch and land-mass that Dryden would have us *imagine* to have occurred under the august and propitious circumstances he describes. Both the stylistic literature in general, then, and earlier sections of this study furnish plentiful examples of iconic syntax in major texts.

If I now include one further, new illustration, I do so at least in part because it represents something of a personal favorite. In writing to Robert Southey in July 1797, Coleridge transcribed an early version of the poem later published as "This Lime-Tree Bower My Prison."[30] As he then wrote it, the poem included the lines:

> My friends . . .
> Wander delighted, and look down, perchance,
> On that same rifted Dell, where many an Ash
> Twists it's [sic] wild limbs beside the ferny rock . . .

In this passage the surface syntactic order of the constituents within each clause corresponds closely to their probable order in deep structure. At the same time we may note in passing Coleridge's use of the verb *twists* in the final clause, a verb which must effectively carry all of the descriptive weight as Coleridge tries to capture for us the ashes' strangely contorted poses.

This original text was not destined to last long. By 1800, when the poem appeared in the *Annual Anthology*, the passage excerpted above had undergone several changes:

> Friends, whom I never more may meet again, . . .
> Wander in gladness, and wind down, perchance,
> To that still roaring dell . . .
> Where its slim trunk the ash from rock to rock
> Flings arching like a bridge;
> (CPW I, 179: 6, 8–9, 12–13)

In comparing these two texts, one may by all means commend Coleridge for his intuition that the poem would benefit from having the imagined walking-party actually "wind down" to the waterfall instead of remaining mere spectators high above it. Much may also be said for the characteristically Coleridgean oxymoron "still roaring" which replaces the relatively drab "same rifted" of the 1797 text. Most relevant to our present concerns, however, are the newly introduced syntactic inversions of lines 12 and 13. In the 1800 revision, two correlative PPs *(from rock* and *to rock)* have been preposed, and the object NP *(its slim trunk)* has also been fronted within its clause. These emendations represent an excellent example of iconically motivated syntactic maneuvering. The contortions of the later text's syntax, to be precise, surely help to convey the twisted form of the ash trees that fill this particular Coleridgean "dell" as they recreate for the reader a linguistic "wild"-ness wholly absent from the syntactically tame early version.

This particular case history differs from others that I have presented in this essay for one very significant reason. For once, it seems to me, the interpretive claim that I have made need not fall back upon a humble appeal for *intuitive* assent.[31] For, in this instance, the poet himself, sensing however unconsciously the expressive power now concentrated in the syntactic form of his newly revised lines, also felt free to replace the (once pivotal) verb *twists* with *flings.* This decision represents in its own right an aesthetically fortunate move in that it adds a new dynamism and brings out a previously unsuspected horizontal axis to the trees' arc over the waterfall. But by and in itself, this verbal emendation could never have been so successful had not Coleridge's syntactic rephrasing of the passage already built convolution into his overall description stylistically. The introduction of *flings* and its success as an ameliorative revision thus offers valuable corroboration for the hypothesis that "twistedness" becomes in the 1800 text of this poem a function of syntactic rather than lexical choice.

In our final example of syntactic iconicity, then, we see an interplay between *"referential* or *propositional* meaning" (the strictly semantic content of the word *twists,* however that is to be determined) and what might be termed *"stylistic* meaning" (in this passage, the iconic expressive power of Coleridge's twisted syntax). By reviewing the variant texts of this poem chronologically, we discover Coleridge's capacity for shifting the weight of his description, so to speak, from one foot to the other. As iconically charged syntactic style assumes a particular semantic function in the transition from the 1797 to the 1800 texts, so Coleridge's need to express that same semantic notion explicitly and referentially appears to diminish.

I am of course well aware that many traditional critical theorists and hard-line transformational grammarians alike will have problems in accepting the idea that syntactic form can "mean" in this very definite, almost paraphrasable sense. A single example such as that presented here will scarcely persuade such skeptics, furthermore, and if we restrict our discussion to cases of interpretive iconicity alone, progress will be slow indeed, since few such cases are so dramatically corroborable using textual emendations as clinching evidence. In what remains of this chapter, therefore, I want to turn instead to a different subfield of interpretive stylistics, an area too seldom discussed by contemporary stylists—*rhetorical* applications of poetic syntax. There, if anywhere, in the use of style as an *overtly* argumentative tool, we should be able to observe and evaluate syntactic forms' power to "mean."

IV

In his satiric poem "The Medall," John Dryden writes:

> The common Cry is ev'n Religion's Test;
> The *Turk's* is, at *Constantinople*, best;
> Idols in *India*, Popery at *Rome*;
> And our own Worship only true at home:
> (WJD II, 46: 103–106)

These four lines offer the reader an inductive generalization (line 103) supported by four items of evidence. In presenting that evidence, Dryden relies on two quite separate techniques to convince his reader that it does indeed provide an adequate basis for the inference he has drawn. He depends first and foremost, of course, on having selected appropriately varied yet complementary illustrations of his thesis. Both geographically and theologically, his four exempla suppose an attractively heterogeneous field of discourse. On these grounds alone, Dryden may hope to carry the day argumentatively, relying only on the simplest semantic interpretation of his lines and on our tacit understanding of common-sense criteria for assessing argument-by-exemplification. If the reader is indeed convinced by these means, he may be said to have accepted what I shall call the *propositional argument* of Dryden's lines.

The syntactic form of lines 104–106, however, and especially the exaggeratedly parallel, gapped clauses of line 105, fuel a subsidiary, entirely *stylistic argument* in the very same passage. Inevitably (and despite the syntactic deletions that have occurred in deriving the precise surface form of these clauses) the reader recognizes Dryden's repeated use of the simple syntactic formula, "A is best/true in/at B." Further, he intuitively defines paradigmatic classes for each of the "variables" in that formula—names of religions to occupy position A; corresponding geographical locations for position B. But in positing this syntactic template, the reader unwittingly helps Dryden to achieve his persuasive goal, for the abstract claim that it embodies ("religion x is best at geographical location x") exactly parallels Dryden's own summary statement in line 103.

Still more interestingly, I think, this crucial if abstract syntactic formula, once established by the reader, actually hints at examples that Dryden has no room to detail ("Shinto is true in Japan" for instance) and even permits modern readers to project corroboratory cases about which Dryden himself could, in principle, have known nothing ("Mormonism is best at Salt Lake City"). Thus the repetitive syntactic form both unifies and universalizes what would otherwise be effective but isolated corroboratory examples.[32]

It is just such a usage of poetic syntax that I wish to term *rhetorical*.[33] In lines like these, syntactic form plays a direct and clearly defined role in developing the poet's argument. Its contribution to the presentation of Dryden's case is so distinct that I was able virtually to paraphrase it propositionally in the paragraph before last. Nor can this particular function of poetic syntax possibly be viewed as either mimetic or iconic. Rather, Dryden's syntactic choices are designed solely to enable him to promote stylistically an argumentative proposition, a thesis consciously conceived and explicitly advanced.

Let me take a moment here to refine the crucial definition that I am proposing. If iconic interpretive correlations connect syntactic choices with a poet's efforts at concrete physical *description,* and if mimesis, as a stylistic strategy, introduces poetic syntax into a broadly *expository* framework, then poets may be said to be using rhetorical syntactic techniques whenever they choose their syntactic form with an eye to furthering essentially *persuasive* ends. The rhetorical application of some technical or perceptual feature of syntactic structure may thus be said to enhance the reader's appreciation of a poet's intended inferences or deductions rather than improving his understanding of the text's immediate denotative content.

I certainly do not lay claim to any great originality in isolating this category of stylistic effects for attention. Dillon, in a paper that I have already cited extensively in this essay, proposes three "modes" of syntactic manipulation: the "prosodic" (an aspect of poetic syntax that I have chosen to yield to the metrists), the "mimetic" (a category that conflates my own iconic and mimetic functions), and what he calls "the presentative."[34] The last-named category, for Dillon, includes principally cases in which Topicalization or PP-Fronting may be used to emphasize or highlight the referents of the syntactic items that they prepose. Corresponding, then, to the parallel examples of mimesis and iconicity offered as sentences (1) and (2) earlier in this chapter, sentence (3) would represent the paradigmatic example of rhetorical or presentative syntax:

> (3) Behind *that* door, ladies and gentlemen, lies tonight's Grand Prize, a 1983 Buick Skylark. (RHETORICAL APPLICATION)

Fronting the PP *behind that door* in this instance does not evolve out of any attempt to mimic physical movement or arrangement, nor does it constitute stylistic simulation of any thematic concern. Indeed, if we avoid all consideration of the specific communicative context, the transformed syntactic structure of the sentence appears motiveless. Only if we deliberately broaden our view to include the speaker/writer's communicative *intent* can we make any sense of the structural frames that he has chosen, as we appreciate his attempt to direct his audience's gaze in a certain way, to delay their discovery of the nature of "tonight's Grand Prize," or most probably to do both these things at once.

Simple rhetorical *emphasis* of this kind, however, Dillon's "presentative mode," always seemed to me a limited and unsophisticated way for great poets to have employed the vast resources of syntax argumentatively. The tendency for past studies of poetic syntax to fall back repeatedly on examples of Topicalization or of PP-Fronting (if indeed they discussed rhetorical applications of syntactic devices at all) might be due, I surmised, to most stylists' preoccupation with the Romantic and post-Romantic periods of English literature, periods in which direct argumentation in poetry was held in relatively low esteem.[35] With this in mind, therefore, I deliberately directed my own attention toward a school of poets whose advocacy of poetic argument has never been in doubt—the Augustans—and in particular toward the widely acknowledged master of that particular genre,

John Dryden. With a variety of cases such as that cited from "The Medall" above, I began to mine a rich vein of rhetorical stylistic effects.

The passages that I shall discuss in the following pages all exemplify, then, Dryden's masterly ability to correlate syntactic form with ratiocinative intent. What distinguishes them from one another are the ways in which the stylistic argument is made to amplify, to coincide with, to throw into question, or even to undercut the propositional argument with which it invariably coexists. (My introductory illustration exemplified only the simplest possible case, in which syntactic argument precisely parallels and reinforces propositional content. But the use of these two terms—indeed the very notion of "stylistic argument" as a concept in its own right—opens up the possibility of far more complex relationships.) We are now in a position to consider a few of these important cases.

The following couplet is taken from what is probably Dryden's best known satire, "Absalom and Achitophel":

> God's pamper'd people whom, debauch'd with ease,
> No King could govern, nor no God could please;
> (WJD II, 7: 47–48)

To determine Dryden's explicit propositional argument in these lines, we need to set them in context. In line 45 the poet first introduced his reader to the Israelites (or, reading the text allegorically, the British public), characterizing them as "a Headstrong, Moody, Murmuring race." Their headstrong nature, he now claims in line 48, appears most blatantly in their political and theological fickleness. Propositionally, therefore, this couplet offers an opinion about the Israelite (British) mob—a simple fact to be borne in mind during the discussion that follows.

Perceptually, the syntactic technique of this couplet differs only trivially if at all from that of the lines from "The Medall" that we discussed above. Line 48 of this poem, to be specific, achieves the same close parallelism seen in line 105 of the other. In the earlier case, it will be recalled, I argued that the general syntactic congruence of the conjoined clauses, together with the semantic similarity of the syntactic items that occupied structurally equivalent positions in them, led the reader to take two interpretively crucial steps. First, the reader reformulates Dryden's overarching generalization about geographical places and the beliefs appropriate to them; then he extends it to embrace a variety of unspecified but logically compatible examples. In so doing, he finds his "stylistic logic" to coincide exactly with Dryden's explicit induction. But in our second case, no such strategy would occur to the reader. Two of the key terms implicitly paired by the syntactic congruence, *govern* and *please*, by no means form a natural semantic class (as for example, did *Constantinople, India,* and *Rome* above). As a result, extending this class of predicates so as to predict a third or a fourth member would be, in a practical sense, impossible.

Let us turn then to the other twosome created by Dryden's choice of parallel syntactic form in line 48—the words *King* and *God.* Once again, of course, the reader seeking a ready-made semantic class to encompass these two items will find himself frustrated. Yet the perceptual parallelism in the line remains a powerful influence, suggesting that the poet may himself see some semantic connection between these two items not apparently deducible from everyday usage.[36] It is this hypothesis, however tentative at first, that ultimately unlocks the full power of Dryden's couplet. For in positing a semantic relationship between these syntactic terms (and thus also between their referents) as the stylistic argument of this passage, the reader rediscovers a major theme of "Absalom and Achitophel"—a theme articulated in both the opening and the closing lines of the poem:

> . . . several Mothers bore
> To *Godlike David*, several Sons before.
> (WJD II, 6: 13–14; emphasis my own)

> Once more the *Godlike David* was Restor'd,
> And willing Nations knew their Lawful Lord.
> (WJD II, 36: 1030–1031; emphasis again mine)

The syntactic form of the couplet we are presently examining reminds the reader, in effect, that this is to be a poem defending the controversial doctrine of the Divine Right of Kings (not just an innocuous paraphrase of a relatively obscure Bible story) and that in daring to attempt yet another change of monarch, the British (Israelites) are defying powers infinitely greater than they at first realize. Of course, the perceptual parallelism in line 48 of the poem advances such a defense of the Stuart cause only indirectly, merely linking the terms *King* and *God* without explicitly equating them. Yet in its context, such a stylistic connection surely takes on the force of an argumentative "proxy," the echo of an argument already expressed more unambiguously elsewhere and all the more powerful here because of its covert stylistic nature.

For we should remember that at the level of propositional content this couplet is concerned with neither monarchs nor deities, let alone constitutional principles. At that level it remains a simple, if biting, indictment of the Israelite (British) character. This absolutely crucial disjunction of propositional and stylistic arguments in the passage stands out more clearly when one observes that Dryden could have leveled his charge of political and religious willfulness in the following only slightly altered words:

> God's pampered people, whom, debauched with ease,
> No king could govern, nor no *church* could please.

What "gets lost in translation" in my reworking of these verses has nothing to do with their propositional content, everything to do with the couplet's stylistic "hidden agenda," its subtle propaganda in support of Charles and James Stuart.

We have now seen two rather different examples of rhetorical syntactic style. In the first, perceptual parallelism suggested a simple semantic generalization precisely supportive of the main argumentative thrust of the passage in which it occurred. In the second, a very similar syntactic form functioned instead to introduce a second *level* of argument, an echo from elsewhere in the poem working apart from, in addition to, even in spite of, the ostensible role of the passage in its persuasive context. This latter possibility, inherently more surprising, certainly calls for further exemplification. Let us turn, therefore, to one of Dryden's most high-minded poems of intellectual debate, "Religio Laici." Here, after all, the cause is one that was dear to Dryden's heart; on the success of his presentation might have depended in large measure the survival of his church and of his political party, not to mention his own career as a professional poet. Here if anywhere we may expect to encounter the full strength of Dryden's persuasive arsenal.

Early in "Religio Laici," Dryden confronts with remarkable candor his greatest single problem in defending a religion of revealed

truth. Such a faith, he explains, holds the acceptance of certain doctrines essential for salvation. Yet many men, women, and children
have been prevented by accidents of birth beyond their control from
ever encountering, let alone accepting, those doctrines. Geographical isolation is only one of several factors that appear to condemn
countless souls to eternal damnation in this way. In the face of what
appears to be arbitrary cruelty on the part of the God that he is called
upon to defend, Dryden apparently falters:

> Of all Objections this indeed is chief
> To startle Reason, stagger frail Belief:
> (WJD II, 115: 184–185)

At first glance, Dryden seems to have conceded this all-important
point virtually without a fight. Worse yet, he would seem to have
done so in a line (line 185) whose syntactic parallelism sinks to the
level of the decorative but semantically tautologous.

Such an interpretation of these lines fails, I believe, to satisfy a
careful reader, who expects here a far less wholesale retreat from
orthodoxy. To see how this might indeed be so, let us reexamine line
185 more closely. Syntactic parallelism and phonological alliteration
do indeed prompt the reader of this line to place the terms *startle*
and *stagger* in a relation of approximate equivalence that is semantically unremarkable. But a similar equation of the nouns *Reason* and
Belief on the grounds of *their* (entirely analogous) structural parallelism immediately strikes the informed reader as a most unexpected
interpretive consequence of the underlying perceptual pattern. No
Augustan poet-philosopher would so easily or carelessly imply an
identity between these two very distinct mental faculties.

If, then, relating together the *lexical items* that occur in congru-
ent positions in these two clauses proves interpretively unhelpful,
perhaps we should instead pair up the parallel *phrasal* constituents,
Reason and *frail Belief*. In that case, we might suppose Dryden's
intended stylistic argument to run something as follows: "Reason is
equivalent to (only) a frail kind of belief." Just as with the example
from "Absalom and Achitophel" discussed earlier, this hypothesis
should immediately strike a familiar chord. The attentive reader
picks up the reverberations of a theme that has sounded throughout
this long, profoundly antirationalist poem. It is a theme, for example,
expressed in the poem's rightly famous opening simile:

Dim, as the borrow'd beams of Moon and Stars
To *lonely, weary, wandring* Travellers,
Is *Reason* to the *Soul:* . . .
And as those nightly Tapers disappear
When Day's bright Lord ascends our Hemisphere;
So pale grows *Reason* at *Religions* sight.
(WJD II, 109: 1–3, 8–10)

As this simile so beautifully expresses (and as the couplet that we are currently examining then reemphasizes nearly two hundred lines later), Dryden views reason as belief's paler, frailer reflection, a source of welcome but ultimately inadequate and purely derivative illumination. This secondary thesis concerning the role of reason in theological argument, then, and not a pompous, despondent, and self-indulgent reiteration of personal reservations about the eternal fate of ignorant heathens, is responsible for the syntactic form of line 185 of Dryden's poem.

Indeed, if read aright, that same line may be seen to point rather dramatically to the fatal flaw in the counsel of doubt and despair that the passage ostensibly (propositionally) expresses. For, Dryden implies in his equation of reason with frail belief, *another* kind of religious conviction, a faith *not* founded on reason alone, will *not* blanch at problems such as those he has presented. The rout of both reason and frail belief, in other words, by no means spells defeat for that more perfect kind of assurance that, as Dryden later goes on to argue, Anglicanism can provide.

In these lines, then, we see another example of stylistic argument working at a tangent to the propositional argument that the text appears to be taking as its primary emphasis. In this case, indeed, that stylistic argument, once deciphered or intuited, influences in important ways the assumptions that we bring to bear on the passage's propositional content itself.

I propose to investigate one final example of syntactic style functioning as an independent argumentative force before drawing a few general conclusions. What distinguishes this case from the others we have discussed is that in this passage Dryden plays off *against one another* his stylistic and his propositional arguments with delightfully comic results. At the climax of Dryden's satiric masterpiece "Mac Flecknoe," the "aged prince" Flecknoe praises his heir-apparent, Shadwell, in supposedly glowing terms:

> Like mine thy gentle numbers feebly creep,
> Thy Tragick Muse gives smiles, thy Comick sleep.
> (WJD II, 59: 197–198)

We are fully familiar now with syntactic parallelism of the kind exhibited in the second line of this couplet. A simple formula, *"Thy ADJECTIVE Muse gives NOUN,"* underlies each of its constituent clauses. But let us again consider the interpretive consequences of this particular parallelism.

Our previous analyses of ratiocinative syntax revolved around the interaction of perceptual parallelism with a rough semantic equivalence—an equivalence either assumed as a given of the standard language (as in the lines from "The Medall") or imposed on the overall interpretation of the passage by the syntactic form itself (as in the citations from "Absalom and Achitophel" and "Religio Laici"). But line 198 of "Mac Flecknoe" does not conform to either pattern, since the adjectives modifying the identical noun subjects of the two parallel conjuncts [*Tragick* and *Comick (Muse)*] are semantically antonymous. As a result, some general interpretive principle dictates, I believe, that we shall expect the same relationship of antonymy to hold between those same two clauses' objects. In effect, for the evident syntactic parallelism to be matched by an *overall* semantic equivalence, one pair of opposites must be counterbalanced by another. Or, to put this same observation still another way, we sense a stylistically inspired need to resolve a semantic chiasmus for which three of the four crucial terms have been explicitly provided:

```
Tragick   smiles   Comick   'X'
---A---    --B---   ---B---  -A-
```

Finally, if semantic criteria dictate in position 'X' some term antonymous to "smiles," the fundamental syntactic parallelism of the clauses equally certainly requires an unmodified plural noun in that position. Under this dual structural pressure, the reader anticipates as the final word in line 198 one of many terms describing emotional reactions appropriate to the genre tragedy such as "tears" or "frowns."

Such a reconstruction of this line, or more precisely of the interpretive consequences of its rhetorical syntax, implicitly attributes to Dryden the intention of ridiculing Shadwell for routinely inspiring in his audiences emotions diametrically opposed to those conventionally appropriate to the announced genres of his plays. Such an allegation, I would maintain, *is indeed* conveyed by the interaction of this couplet's syntax with its semantics; the indictment of Shadwell would be far weaker than in fact it is were we not thus led up Dryden's stylistic "garden path." But on the surface, Dryden astutely interrupts the apparently determined flow of his own line. He fills the all-important position 'X' in the chiastic sequence diagrammed above with the noun *sleep.* Even as the implicit *stylistic* argument presses us to expect *tears* at the close of line 198, then, explicit *propositional* semantics insist that we add to the list of Dryden's charges against poor Shadwell one further, telling count—that of dullness.

In its context at the frenzied climax of "Mac Flecknoe" this heavily ironic strategy creates a rich variety of comic effects. It is, for instance, Shadwell's ultimate indignity that he is denied even the chance of pleading that his dramatic—or melodramatic—gifts are substantial, his failures simply the result of their misapplication. Far from merely inverting tragedy and comedy in such a straightforward sense, Dryden explains, Shadwell confounds both in a sense-benumbing hodgepodge of absurdities. Correspondingly, it is his mentor Flecknoe's sad fate, as ever, that the paean of praise that he originally intended should turn out to be both backhanded *and* inept, displaying in its clumsy two-level insult that special combination of "Impudence" and "Ignorance" that he had earlier "recommended" to his successor (line 146). For all this satiric richness to be fully effective, however, it is essential to Dryden's stylistic method that the reader of lines 197–198 first appreciate the role of his rhetorical syntax, syntax which both undercuts and is in its turn undercut by the more prosaic terms of the ongoing literary indictment.

V

In the previous section, I attempted to indicate, however summarily, the expressive potential locked inside the syntax of Dryden's famed heroic couplets. On the one hand, such analyses carry a considerable weight of implication for Dryden studies in general. On the other, they significantly broaden the horizon for students of stylistic criticism.

A very high degree of critical consensus surrounds Dryden's role in the history of English versification:

> It is the story of a poet who inherited a medium, perfected it, . . . and handed it on.[37]

Dryden figures consistently as the inventor of the heroic couplet, although, as in this quotation, concern generally centers not so much on his own poetic writings as on those of his predecessors and successors. Dryden's own role, in fact, is generally reduced to that of a talented intermediary who adapted the methods and discoveries of the former to the needs of the latter. Within these rather narrow limits, agreement is the order of the day. George Williamson identifies Dryden's source, the "informing force of the couplet," he says, being "ultimately derived from Latin rhetoric."[38] Critics such as Lillian Feder and K. G. Hamilton then accept that attribution, and proceed to catalog in more detail the specific avenues by which the tradition descended from the classical authors to Dryden himself. And if the origins of the heroic couplet that Dryden "inherited," and of the syntactic norms that accompanied it, are thus supposedly well enough understood to require only the briefest discussion, so too are the features of his technique that particularly attracted the later Neoclassical poets to whom he "handed it on." Dryden's couplets, Hamilton points out, required "a fine organization of words, . . . which in the hands of Pope became an almost geometric manipulation."[39] And this time it is Williamson who concurs, alleging that in the later poet's style syntactic antithesis became "structural rather than significant" and "passed into the very design of the verse."[40]

It is at this point that we may begin to notice critics' apparent aversion to discussing one facet of their topic which one would expect *prima facie* to be of considerable interest and concern. Dryden, they all agree, differs from Pope precisely in his rejection of *excessive* or *pervasive* syntactic balance—*purely* "structural" or "geometric" arrangements. "The extreme compression and strict organization of Pope is not essential to his [Dryden's] method," reiterates Hamilton[41]; Paul Ramsey agrees: "it is easy to overrate their importance in Dryden's poetry."[42] Yet amid all this testimony to the effect that Dryden's heroic couplets were designed to perform some *substantive* poetic function distinct from, and often more highly valued than, the verbal fireworks typical of Pope's style, no voice is to be heard explaining precisely what that function might be. Certainly, excellent studies of individual passages have been published; both Hamilton and Ramsey analyze the style of "Absalom and Achitophel" with considerable success.[43] Such achievements, however, still leave the broader theoretical questions unanswered—and indeed even unasked. What in general terms did Dryden himself expect syntax to contribute toward poetic expression? And how did he bring about such a contribution in his own works in particular?

Thanks to the interpretive stylistic analyses of particular passages undertaken earlier in this chapter, we now find ourselves in a position to begin to formulate answers to these questions. It would, I suspect, be *possible* to distinguish Dryden's heroic couplet style from Pope's perceptually, perhaps as a function of the density or complexity of the syntactic patterns that each employs. No such measure, however, will be very successful, I suspect, in isolating for the experienced reader the touchstone of either poet's genius. It will be far more intuitively satisfying, in the final analysis, to rely instead on the interpretive purposefulness, the intensely directed suasive force, of Dryden's syntactic forms as the characteristic most peculiar to his individual style. For it is this that one always remembers most clearly from reading his work. What for Pope was to become too often mere frosting on the poetic cake is for Dryden an essential ingredient which lends spice and texture to his already tangy argumentative batter. In the analysis of their interpretive application, therefore, rather than in the mere description of Dryden's perceptual patterns themselves, we can come to understand better the character of this major English poet.

Stylistic critics, too, can benefit from discussions such as those in section IV of this chapter, as their theories and methods flex to meet challenges posed by data as fresh and as unfamiliar as the Augustan couplets considered there. At the very least, our discussion of Dryden's poetic syntax has demonstrated conclusively that those familiar stylist's standbys, mimesis and iconicity, fall seriously short of accommodating all of the relationships that may connect syntactic form with literary meaning. Nor can the "emphatic" function be any longer regarded as the sole, or even as the major, *rhetorical* interpretive strategy. We clearly need a new language altogether to help us capture the delicate nuances possible where syntactic style is employed to enhance argument, persuasion, and logic.

Implicitly, I have already hinted at one direction that future discussions in this area might take. Rhetorical strategies might, I suspect, be usefully classified on the basis of the kind of impact "stylistic argument" has on "propositional content." To call an effect "corroborative," for example, might entail that one was claiming a parallelism to exist between the thrusts of these two aspects of the argument of the passage under discussion. "Ironic" strategies would, by contrast, involve one facet of the argument undercutting the other. And "displaced" rhetorical strategies would occur wherever a stylistic argument picked up an argumentative thesis propounded propositionally not in the same passage but elsewhere in the text.

Such details will take considerable time to refine; I have done no more than scratch the surface in this chapter. What is important, I believe, is that these questions be raised, for stylists have two major responsibilities in the subfield of interpretive stylistics at the present stage of its evolution. The first is to affirm (and to reaffirm until it is clearly understood) that stylistic criticism pursues correlations between syntactic forms and their specific interpretation within the unique framework of a given text, not some linguistic passkey to the literature of the world. The second, equally vital, is to acknowledge and admire the richness and variety of those correlations. If all that I have achieved in these pages is to contribute to the "hunt" in which we are all engaged a few interpretive "possums" from a family whose presence was heretofore barely even suspected, then I still hold that effort alone to have been well worthwhile.

CHAPTER FIVE

Conclusions Theoretical and Pedagogical

Stylistics is . . . a dialogue between literary reader and
linguistic observer, in which insight, not mere objectivity, is the goal.
    —Geoffrey Leech and Michael Short, *Style in*
Fiction.

I

In chapter 1 of this study I outlined some criteria by which I
anticipated that my discussion of syntactic stylistics would, explicitly
or implicitly, be judged. As an analytical description of a certain set
of data, I suggested, the model I advanced would have to be clearly
articulated and unambiguous in its claims and predictions. I would
have to make every effort to apply it directly to relevant literary
examples. Finally, I should also seek to examine its implications outside the field of stylistics as such. The first two of these three announced goals I would claim already to have attained. Beginning in
chapter 2, I sketched, sometimes in fine detail but more often with
broad strokes, my theory of syntactic stylistics, a theory that I believe
can clarify and enrich debate in both critical and linguistic studies.
In the process I also undertook a variety of textual analyses illustrating my proposals. It remains now only to review that theoretical
model as a whole and to assess its applicability to disciplines less
integrally connected with the academic study of literary works.

As Figure 23 indicates, I claim that stylistic generalizations fall
into three broad classes. *Technical* commentary allies itself closely
with contemporary linguistics, borrowing both its terminology and
its analytical principles from the most widely accepted current versions of syntactic theory. To linguistics it contributes in its turn formal accounts of significant nonstandard literary "dialects." As just

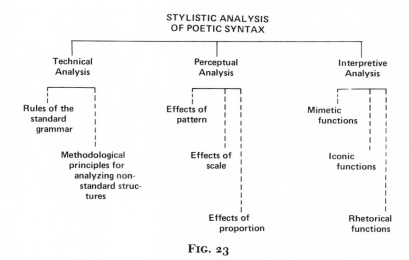

FIG. 23

one of the three subdisciplines embraced by syntactic stylistics, technical analysis stands out as an undeniably scientific pursuit; the stylist's technical claims represent precise hypotheses with empirically testable consequences. (As we shall shortly see, the same cannot be said so confidently, if at all, for the other branches of the discipline, nor, therefore, for syntactic stylistics as a whole.)

Orthodox syntactic theory includes no aesthetic component. Any stylistic judgments, therefore, that draw on aesthetic concepts must by definition belong in some category other than the technical. *Perceptual* stylistic analysis, as I have called it, arises from just such an application of general aesthetic principles to linguistic material. To the extent that the study of aesthetics itself can be systematized, perceptual stylistics will approach technical stylistics in its rigor and theoretical precision. Its raw materials, however, will never overlap with those designated for technical description, since notions such as "balance," "antithesis," and "delay" have no role to play in that aspect of language captured by traditional syntactic theories.

Interpretive stylistics differs fundamentally from both technical and perceptual analysis. In this subfield, the stylist draws on either of the other two subfields (or on them both) to provide one side of a delicate balance, as he links syntactic form, however tenuously, with what he understands of poetic meaning. It is ironic, of course, that this treacherous domain of interpretation should represent both the goal of most stylists' work that carries the greatest popular appeal and that area in which they venture furthest from their roots, furthest from the relatively "safe" territory of technical description. Yet in this respect stylists share their temerity with critics of many other persuasions—biographers, historians, and psychoanalysts, for example, all of whom eventually find themselves forced to lay aside their respective specializations and to make unambiguous *critical* claims about a specific literary text. To the extent that stylistics rests at least one leg of its argument on linguistic bedrock, on fundamental claims about a central aspect of every text's form—the common core of meaning contained in its language—to that extent at least the interpretive stylist enjoys as good a chance as anyone of promoting for himself and for a wider audience his critical insights into a given work.

As I have summarized it here, and as I developed it throughout the first four chapters of this study, my theory of syntactic stylistics is just that: an analytical description of an intellectual discipline. I have attempted, that is, to examine what stylists do and to discover how they do it. Keeping in mind the distinctions I have drawn among types of stylistic statement should make it easier for readers to determine whether particular stylists have compatible or incompatible views on a particular passage, where those views diverge, and what kinds of evidence might decide between them. Conversely, my model should also help to isolate "nonarguments" in stylistics, debates in which the parties involved mistakenly believe themselves to be at odds while their analyses actually differ so radically in assumptions and materials that rational discussion is effectively impossible. Finally, I hope that my enumeration of areas of legitimate stylistic comment may help to prompt textual analyses where none were considered before, analyses which may lead us to either extend or restrict the specific taxonomy that I have proposed. All of these potential developments I see as proper and indeed desirable consequences of my proposals.

At a number of points earlier in this study, though, I was careful to point with concern to other possible interpretations or applications of my theory which I viewed as *illegitimate.* Among the most potentially damaging, I would number, first, the assumption that this theory might be either a theory of reading or an account of the process of poetic composition, and, second, the completely independent suspicion that the whole activity might conceal a pernicious system for evaluating the merit of a given work of literature. It is important now to sweep these two theoretical minefields with proper care.

In no sense, first of all, have I attempted here to characterize the process by which anyone actually reads a work of literature.[1] My concern has been with justifying an interpretation rather than with reaching one, with intellectual evaluation rather than with heuristic experimentation. Nor is this assertion, which I make with some insistence, in any way compromised by the fact that I have frequently made reference to "the reader" in the course of my analyses.

W. Daniel Wilson recently deplored the "unruly profuseness," the "tangled mass" of epithets currently applied by critics to the once innocent "reader," the "jargonistic neologisms" of what has come to be called the "reader-response school" of critical theory.[2] In a wide-ranging study, he reviewed the content, whether stated or only implied, of such terminological monstrosities as the "narratee" (Gerald Prince), the "optimum reader" (Lowry Nelson, Jr.), and the "addressee" (Manfred Naumann). Fortunately for the uninitiated, Wilson's final conclusion is that, sensitively interpreted, just three terms adequately characterize the only important and theoretically distinguishable figures postulated by reader-response theorists. *"Characterized* fictive readers" exist entirely within the text, as for example do the thoroughly exaggerated figures with whom Tristram Shandy carries on a constant dialog in Laurence Sterne's novel of the same name. *"Implied* fictive readers," though no less creatures of the text, cannot be used ironically or satirically in the same way. Intimately linked to "our overall interpretation" of a given work, they embody "the attitudes and judgments demanded of the real reader by the text."[3] Critics generally agree, for example, that one capacity essential to a fully adequate reading of *Tristram Shandy* is the capacity to laugh *with* Sterne himself *at* the more absurd of the "characterized readers" he presents in the course of his rambling narration. Insofar as this ability is actually demanded of the reader of this novel, it will define in one important respect the work's "implied readership."

"Both these fictive readers," fictive in the straightforward sense that they exist solely by virtue of the fictional texts to which they are uniquely relevant, "must be distinguished from real readers," Wilson then goes on to claim, ". . . even if real readers actualize the implied reader's role after the work is created."[4] Wilson's theory thus leaves us with just three kinds of "reader": the characterized, the implied, and the real. Alas, wherever in the preceding pages *I* have used the term "the reader," I have been referring to *none* of these theoretical entities, but to a fourth, a figure that I shall tentatively call the *"native* reader."[5]

As the name is supposed to suggest, the native reader bears much the same relation to stylistic theory that the "native speaker/ hearer" has traditionally borne to transformational linguistic theory and rests on a series of abstractions and simplifications of individual events inescapable if one wishes stylistic theory to achieve a high level of what Noam Chomsky would term "descriptive power." Major advances in *linguistics* became possible after Chomsky advocated temporarily putting to one side the attested linguistic behavior of individual informants and taking as data instead what all speakers of a given language seemed to agree to be the intuitive core of their linguistic knowledge. My introduction of the native reader depends on a precisely analogous conscious idealization in *stylistic* studies.[6] In itself this step has been justified, I would maintain, by the critical and technical insights that this study has been able to achieve. Where such practical advantages do not seem to accrue from positing my particular brand of native reader, however, the assumptions that the term encodes are easily undone or held in abeyance.

As a necessary condition for the stylistic theory that it enables, but also paradoxically as a creature of that theory, the concept of the native reader involves specific idealizations in *each* of the areas addressed by my analytical model. Since technical stylistics depends heavily on linguistic theory, as has been argued several times, a rather straightforward assumption for us to make is that one component, so to speak, of my native reader will in fact be the linguist's native speaker/hearer. Idealization in the technical sphere is thus virtually defined *a priori.* To complete a fully adequate characterization of the native reader, though, would also require parallel abstractions in the perceptual and even the interpretive subfields, where a consensus on what material should be regarded as idiosyncratic and on methods for achieving appropriate generalizations is far less likely to be forthcoming.

Fortunately, if the general logic underlying my development of a native readership is accepted, then it may prove unnecessary ever to formulate such criteria precisely; a "complete characterization" may be exactly what is *not* called for. For, as I argued in chapter 1, to isolate the native reader from the specific stylistic case that he "feeds" immediately implies for him an extratheoretical reality that endangers his very usefulness. I find myself increasingly convinced, therefore, that the generalizations one makes about "the reader" in the course of a stylistic analysis are ultimately justified *en bloc* by the critical insights they promote. Certainly, losses may be incurred as a result of this process of idealization, and Stanley Fish and Barbara Herrnstein Smith are right to demand that we be alert for such "slippage." But as Paul Armstrong notes, this problem is not unique to stylistics:

> [Every] hermeneutic standpoint has its own dialectic of blindness and insight—a ratio of disguise and disclosure that stems from its presuppositions. To accept a method of interpretation is to . . . gamble . . . that the insight its assumptions make possible will offset the risk of blindness.[7]

Detailed caviling about excessively (or inadequately) sophisticated claims that some stylist may have made for the reader he assumed when constructing his argument thus misses the mark unless the caviler also addresses what Armstrong calls the criterion of "efficacy,"[8] the overall gains or losses that have resulted for our understanding of the text under discussion or for our grasp of the role of language in literature as a whole.

It is of course precisely this flexibility, which I view as inherent in this field of scholarship, that leads me to believe that the procedural obstacles that Fish creates for himself and for stylistics as a discipline in his more recent essays are mere mirages. Fish argues himself into a position where he can no longer live with idealized abstractions (although he used them repeatedly in his earlier work with most impressive results). The "interpretive community," as I noted in chapter 1, then represents Fish's belated attempt to resurrect on a different plane that idealization on which his best critical work always depended. He tries to remove his idealized reader from the realm of stylistic theory altogether, and to base that construct instead on sociocultural and general linguistic criteria. Inevitably, this attempt fails since all language "communities" fragment finally into individual speakers, our concepts of "dialect" and "language" themselves resting on pre-theoretical abstractions designed for the sole purpose of facilitating linguistic investigation. The interpretive community, analogously, can exist only as part of a stylistic theory, not independently of it. The end justifying the means, to put it bluntly, is what Fish finds unpalatable, and in the final analysis one has simply to decide whether Fish's scruples in this area are one's own.

An altogether different consideration separates my native reader from the reader implied by George Dillon in *his* latest work. In the preceding chapters, I offered an account of what I might call the native reader's "stylistic competence." Dillon, by his own admission, details instead a theory of stylistics based on performance factors—heuristics, pragmatics, and strategies. His theory and my own are thus not incompatible; both assume an idealized reader whose stylistic capabilities can be described or modeled along linguistic lines.

Both may also, in passing, improve our understanding of (though neither of them sets out directly to describe) what Wilson would call the "real reader." To cite just a single example of how, Fish notwithstanding, this may be so, recall that in the closing paragraphs of chapter 2 I promised further discussion of the role played by nonstandard coordinate structure deletions in Pope's poetry. That promise followed hard on the heels of an extended theoretical argument. I had proposed specifically that an adequate technical account of Augustan poetic syntax would have to include some statement to the effect that all coordinate structure deletion rules apply freely (that is, in either direction) in texts of this period, uncontrolled by the constraints that affect such processes in standard modern English. This theoretical hypothesis, I argued, easily won out over reliance on a series of other (*individually* no more radical) analyses that would each explain only a subset of the attested cases of syntactic irregularity. For it permitted the stylist to capture a major generalization by uniting several phenomena that must otherwise be assumed to appear together in Augustan poetry by a most extreme coincidence.

My own informal observations, which several audiences at professional meetings have not found cause to dispute, suggest that we may derive some circumstantial evidence in favor of this purely theoretical technical argument from the literature classroom.[9] When first introduced to Augustan poetry, most students encounter some difficulty with its syntax. They claim "not to understand" passages whose vocabulary and overall interpretation are relatively straightforward; yet when one disentangles for them the poetic inversions and deletions with which the text is riddled, they routinely admit that the whole is now perfectly clear. What is striking, however, is not merely the fact that syntax should provide the major stumbling block to these students, but the manner in which, in due course, they overcome their hesitancy. Rather than comprehending one line, or even one construction at a time, that is, they almost always struggle along for some time, then suddenly find themselves able to interpret all of the text equally well.

If we assume for a moment that this "informal observation" on my part could be adequately corroborated—a feat which, to my mind, would raise the assessment of "reader-response" to new heights—then the following conclusion would flow from it rather naturally. The available pedagogical evidence would be fully compatible with my own stylistic hypothesis about coordinate structure deletions in Pope's poetry. My technical analysis requires that only one very general statement predict a rather large variety of nonstandard constructions. If this happens also to be the correct way to look at things *practically,* then we might expect that for each student mastery of one such construction would entail mastery of all, creating a sort of "threshold" effect in terms of reading strategies of the kind discussed by Dillon in his recent book. Conversely, while my observations of classroom behavior do not absolutely conflict with the alternative, multiple-rule theoretical hypothesis, accommodating those two bodies of data to one another would seem to force us to assume that several disparate syntactic processes just happen to be learned simultaneously by inexperienced readers—a coincidence that would compound the coincidence already noted from a purely theoretical standpoint above.[10]

Let me note in closing that stylistics would certainly benefit from many more such technical analyses and from correlations of those analyses with teachers' problems and teachers' solutions to those problems. I see every reason to hope that, with enough of this detailed information, stylistics as a discipline may help to improve the teaching of literary comprehension. A full discussion of this and of the many other potential applications of my stylistic theory in "the real world" deserves, however, far more extensive treatment than I can afford it here.

The implications of my theory of stylistics for our assessment of the way in which readers read constitute fertile soil for debate. While mine is not a theory *of* reading, one might summarize, it certainly has some points to make *about* reading. It requires little ingenuity, then, to estimate from the preceding discussion my opinion of how far stylistic theory should venture in making statements about how poets write. The stylist, I would claim, need make little (or even no) reference to the poet in assembling his critical case. Such references as are made will generally be matters of critical cliche, and will be made with due regard for the danger of attributing too definite a profile to a specific historical figure on the basis of stylistic data alone. A stylistic argument that sets forth truly original and substantive claims about the psyche of the poet whose works it discusses should be viewed with some caution.

Not that interesting observations can never be made in this general area. Richard Ohmann's *Shaw: The Style and the Man* certainly indulges in some psychological speculation, but Ohmann avoids major problems by openly coupling a stylistic analysis of Shaw's prose with an *independently* validated psychoanalytical study of Shaw the man. My own analysis in an early paper of Wordsworth's textual revisions in *The Ruined Cottage* similarly toyed with psychoanalytical reconstruction.[11] My comments too, however, involved corroborating stylistically some general trends in Wordsworth's philosophical thought that are almost universally accepted. What the stylist must avoid is emerging as a closet analyst or closet biographer, proposing his own character sketches or disputing those of others solely on the basis of his linguistically grounded observations. This risk can be avoided, providing that, as always, we delimit clearly the legitimate scope of stylistic commentary and draw a precise line setting stylistic judgments apart from the psychobiographical information with which we may later associate them. Only within such a framework will the poet assume the correct degree of prominence in stylistic theory as an intriguing but by no means integral aspect of the stylist's work.

The third and last of my caveats against potential abuses of my stylistic theory concerns the question of evaluative assessment. As I remarked early in chapter 4, E. L. Epstein, in his essay "The Self-Reflexive Artefact," sets about integrating a single stylistic concept (mimesis) into a comprehensive overview of the most highly rated literary works from different historical periods. He hypothesizes that mimesis represents the interpretive function of poetic syntax most favored by readers and critics alike during the past two centuries, a conclusion with which, in such very general terms, I would probably want to concur. It is vital to bear in mind, though, that Epstein's is an essentially observational hypothesis, which describes as accurately as possible a historical state of affairs rather than prescribing some absolute, right-minded criterion of excellence for current or future readers. In terms of its impact on the casual reader, his argument still suffers from two serious practical drawbacks. First, Epstein assumes that we have in place a stylistic model sufficiently sensitive to be relied on when gathering the stylistic data so crucial to his correlation of them with evaluative norms. In the event, my own foray into Dryden's rhetorical style has shown all too clearly the inadequacies of our current understanding of interpretive strategies in general. We cannot, then, be sure that the works Epstein points to as critically preferred do in fact share the common basis in interpretive effect that he claims for them. Second, Epstein also accepts too easily, I think, the possibility of separating readers' stylistic evaluation of a text from their assessment of its genre, its philosophy, or even its politics. In short, we need a far more sophisticated stylistic theory than is currently available, not to mention a clearer understanding of the notion of the literary "canon," before the link between style and literary value can be authoritatively established.

Above all, it must be reemphasized that no aspect of the theory presented in these pages translates straightforwardly into an algorithm for plotting the worth of a given work. Mimesis does not outrank iconicity on some cosmic scale of values; a text that exhibits both perceptual *and* technical features worthy of analysis is not thereby more noteworthy than one that is, say, technically unexceptional. We are simply a very long way from appreciating fully the role that syntactic style plays in the apportionment of general critical acclaim—a process that must be, to say the least, exceedingly complex.

II

The contentious state of modern critical theory may be blamed for the rather negative tone and defensive thinking of this final chapter. These same features, however, cannot be allowed to prevail to the very end of the study. Stylistic analysis is emerging from a period of some disarray; it remains in need of considerable repair. But it also offers great hope for a positive and productive future. Like its fellow-traveler, linguistic theory, stylistics finds itself at a crossroads, exhausted by the rapid progress of the sixties and the seventies yet uncertain of where the eighties will lead. This air of indecision by no means entails that no road forward can be discerned; on the contrary, the discipline simply needs to reorient itself, to reexamine its bases and goals, and to gather its energies before setting forward once again. This study has attempted to begin such a revitalization. By reviewing the arguments of some of stylistics' major detractors, I have shown the comparative insubstantiality of their reservations; by analyzing many different passages of poetry, I have suggested a series of avenues for further investigation. But the real excitement still lies ahead, in the work yet to be done developing what must surely become a comprehensive and critically invaluable theory of syntactic stylistics.

Notes

1. A Theory of Poetic Syntax

1. Roman Jakobson, "Linguistics and Poetics," in *Style in Language,* ed. Thomas A. Sebeok (Cambridge: MIT Press, 1960); rpt. in *Essays on the Language of Literature,* ed. Seymour Chatman and Samuel R. Levin (Boston: Houghton Mifflin, 1967), p. 322.

2. M. A. K. Halliday, "Descriptive Linguistics in Literary Studies," in *English Studies Today,* ed. G. I. Duthie (Edinburgh: Edinburgh University Press, 1964); rpt. in *Linguistics and Literary Style,* ed. Donald C. Freeman (New York: Holt Rinehart & Winston, 1970), p. 70.

3. Seymour Chatman, "Milton's Participial Style," *PMLA* 83 (1968), 1398.

4. Donald C. Freeman, "The Strategy of Fusion: Dylan Thomas's Syntax," in *Style and Structure in Literature: Essays in the New Stylistics,* ed. Roger Fowler (Ithaca, N.Y.: Cornell University Press, 1975), pp. 19–39.

5. Jacques Derrida, "Signature Event Context," *Glyph* 1 (1977), 174.

6. Ibid., p. 189.

7. E. D. Hirsch, *Validity in Interpretation* (New Haven and London: Yale University Press, 1967), p. 170.

8. Ibid., p. 17.

9. Ibid., p. 169.

10. Ibid., p. 173.

11. For another contribution to this debate, see Barbara Herrnstein Smith, *On the Margins of Discourse: The Relation of Literature to Language* (Chicago and London: University of Chicago Press, 1978), p. 33.

12. Jacques Derrida, "Limited Inc.: a b c . . . ," *Glyph* 2 (1978), 168.

13. This because Derrida is certainly anxious that the consequences of his reexamination of the linguistic code be extended to the analysis of spoken language. Historically, Derrida's immediate target happened to involve written forms and thus also literature. It was for this reason that stylists rather than theoretical linguists found themselves facing the unwelcome task of rebutting the deconstructionists' attacks.

The best-known exception to this generalization, an exchange between Derrida and speech-act theorist John R. Searle in the pages of *Glyph,* demonstrates all too clearly the inability of theoretical linguists themselves to take seriously and to meet *on its own ground* the challenge of a Derridean critique (see Derrida, "Signature Event Context," and "Limited Inc."; and John R. Searle, "Reiterating the Differences: A Reply to Derrida," *Glyph* 1 [1977], 198–208).

14. Noam Chomsky, *Syntactic Structures* (The Hague: Mouton, 1957), p. 50.

15. Ibid., p. 56.

16. Noam Chomsky, *Language and Mind* (New York: Harcourt Brace Jovanovich, 1972), p. 26.

17. See Paul B. Armstrong, "The Conflict of Interpretations and the Limits of Pluralism," *PMLA* 98 (1983), 344–345.

18. Frank Kermode, *The Sense of an Ending* (New York: Oxford University Press, 1967). Contrast here Smith, pp. 9–13 and chap. 2.

19. Stanley Fish, *Is There A Text In This Class?* (Cambridge and London: Harvard University Press, 1980), pp. 239, 242; the term "shared pretense" is borrowed from Searle.

20. Ibid., p. 72.

21. Richard Ohmann, *Shaw: The Style and the Man* (Middletown, Conn.: Wesleyan University Press, 1962); Seymour Chatman, *The Later Style of Henry James* (Oxford: Blackwells Press, 1972).

22. See for instance Donald C. Freeman, "Literature as Property: A Review Article," *Language and Style* 13:2 (1980), 156–173.

23. Fish, p. 150.

24. Ibid., p. 169. As Paul Armstrong notes, Fish comes even closer "to vicious circularity" in his dispute with John Reichert (see Fish, p. 299, cited in Armstrong, p. 346).

25. Ibid., pp. 155–158.

26. Ibid., p. 318.

27. Ibid., p. 28.

28. Ibid., p. 370. Gerald Graff also attacks Fish's interpretive communities in *Literature Against Itself* (Chicago and London: University of Chicago Press, 1979), pp. 166–168. His note to p. 168 cites several other discussions of Fish's position.

29. See for example Seymour Chatman and Samuel R. Levin, eds., *Essays on the Language of Literature* (Boston: Houghton Mifflin, 1967); Roger Fowler, ed., *Style and Structure in Literature: Essays in the New Stylistics* (Ithaca, N.Y.: Cornell University Press, 1975); and Donald C. Freeman, ed., *Linguistics and Literary Style* (New York: Holt Rinehart & Winston, 1970) and *Essays in Modern Stylistics* (London and New York: Methuen, 1981).

30. I think in particular of Josephine Miles, *Eras and Modes in English Poetry* (Berkeley and Los Angeles: University of California Press, 1957); Morris Halle and S. Jay Keyser, *English Stress: Its Form, Its Growth, and Its Role in Verse* (New York: Harper & Row, 1971); George L. Dillon, *Language Processing and the Reading of Literature: Toward a Model of Comprehension* (Bloomington and London: Indiana University Press, 1978); and Mary Louise Pratt, *Toward a Speech Act Theory of Discourse* (Bloomington and London: Indiana University Press, 1977), respectively.

Students of poetic syntax, incidentally, might learn a great deal from reflecting on the success of these volumes. Almost immediately upon publication each of these texts significantly raised the level of intellectual debate in its respective subfield. The provision of a basic framework for discussion has led quite naturally to the development of more questions and to the evolution of a still more sophisticated theoretical model. There is thus every reason to hope for an equal measure of success to attend the formulation of a comprehensive theory of poetic syntax.

31. Dillon, p. xvi.

32. Ibid., p. xxvii.

33. For a definition and discussion of the terms "competence" and "performance," see Noam Chomsky, *Aspects of the Theory of Syntax* (Cambridge: MIT Press, 1965), pp. 3–15.

34. See, for instance, Susumu Kuno, "The Position of Relative Clauses and Conjunctions," *Linguistic Inquiry* 5:1 (1974), 117–136.

35. In what follows, I shall use the term "linguistic competence" to refer to the whole of this field of shared analytical assumptions, except when, for a specific purpose, I wish to distinguish between exclusively language-oriented cognitive skills and those with broader applicability.

36. Fish, chap. 6.

37. Ibid., pp. 303–304; italics mine.

38. Jonathan Culler, *Structuralist Poetics* (London and Ithaca, N.Y.: Routledge & Kegan Paul and Cornell University Press, 1975), p. 114.

39. Thus Smith's criticisms of stylistics, which we shall consider in some detail in chap. 4, figure in her book as the second barrel of an attack which takes as its first target contemporary syntactic theory as a whole: "The professional linguist's . . . description of the utterance reflects an arbitrary demarcation and abstraction from the fullness, the density, and the spatial, temporal, and causal continuity of all human action and all events in nature" (p. 18).

40. E. R. Steinberg, "Stylistics as a Humanistic Discipline," *Style* 10:1 (1976), 67–78.

41. Timothy R. Austin, "Prolegomenon to a Theory of Comparative Poetic Syntax," *Language and Style* 16 (1983), 433–455.

42. Pratt, p. 26.

43. For an excellent (if terminologically complex) discussion of prose style from a standpoint broadly compatible with my own, see Geoffrey N. Leech and Michael H. Short, *Style in Fiction: A Linguistic Introduction to English Fictional Prose* (London and New York: Longman, 1981).

2. The Technical Analysis of a Literary Text

1. Culler, p. 5.

2. John Reichert, *Making Sense of Literature* (Chicago and London: University of Chicago Press, 1977), p. 24.

3. I must myself plead guilty to having mistaken one kind of argument for the other in a previous paper [see Timothy R. Austin, "Constraints on Syntactic Rules and the Style of Shelley's 'Adonais': An Exercise in Stylistic Criticism," *PTL* 4 (1979), 335–337]. I am grateful to Steven Lapointe for insisting that I reconsider that position.

4. Pratt, p. 16.

5. Ibid., p. 11.

6. Paul Kiparsky, "The Role of Linguistics in a Theory of Poetry," *Daedalus* 102 (1973), 234; rpt. in *Essays in Modern Stylistics*, ed. Donald C. Freeman (London and New York: Methuen, 1981). p. 13.

7. Ibid., p. 243.

8. For a very clear philosophical discussion of this problem of hypotheses' instability and the effects of this problem on the establishment of valid scientificstatements,seeHilaryPutnam,*Mind, Language and Reality: Philosophical Papers, Volume 2* (Cambridge: Cambridge University Press, 1975), pp. 28–30.

9. Leonard Bloomfield, *Language* (London: George Allen & Unwin, 1935), pp. 194–197.

10. Emmon Bach, *Syntactic Theory* (New York: Holt Rinehart & Winston, 1974) contains an excellent bibliography, as also does Adrian Akmajian and Frank Heny, *An Introduction to the Principles of Transformational Syntax* (Cambridge and London: MIT Press, 1975). See also Joan W. Bresnan, "On Complementizers: Toward a Syntactic Theory of Complement Types," *Foundations of Language* 6 (1970), 297–321; Chomsky, *Aspects*, "Conditions on Transformations," in *A Festschrift for Morris Halle*, ed. Stephen R. Anderson and Paul Kiparsky (New York: Holt Rinehart & Winston, 1973), pp. 232–286, and *Reflections on Language* (New York: Pantheon Books, 1975); Joseph E. Emonds, *A Transformational Approach to English Syntax* (New York: Academic Press, 1976); Ray Jackendoff, *Semantic Interpretation in Generative Grammar* (Cambridge and London: MIT Press, 1972), and "Morphological and Semantic Regularities in the Lexicon," *Language* 51 (1975), 639–671;andJohnR.Ross,*Constraints on Variables in Syntax*, Diss. M. I. T., 1967.

11. Bresnan, "A Realistic Transformational Grammar," in *Linguistic Theory and Psychological Reality*, ed. Morris Halle, Joan Bresnan, and George A. Miller (Cambridge and London: MIT Press, 1978), p. 4.

12. Ibid., p. 59.

13. Ibid., p. 4.

14. As in Bloomfield, p. 161.

15. This structure has been simplified to omit any reference to the syntactic "trace" left by the movement rule that has applied (see Chomsky, "Conditions"). While by no means trivial to the EST in general, traces will not substantially affect the analyses presented in the course of this particular study. I shall therefore continue to omit them from tree-structures without further comment.

16. Again see Chomsky, "Conditions," and Emmon Bach and George M. Horn, "Remarks on 'Conditions on Transformations,'" *Linguistic Inquiry* 7:2 (1976), 265–299.

17. The term *filter* is often used in such cases [as in Noam Chomsky and Howard Lasnik, "Filters and Control," *Linguistic Inquiry* 8 (1977), 425–504; see especially pp. 430–433]. However, usage of the three terms *condition, constraint*, and *filter* still tends to be somewhat imprecise.

18. "[T]he great weakness of the theory of transformational grammar is

its enormous descriptive power," [Noam Chomsky, "Some Empirical Issues in the Theory of Transformational Grammar," in *Goals of Linguistic Theory*, ed. Stanley Peters (Englewood Cliffs, N.J.: Prentice-Hall, 1972)]. See also Chomsky and Lasnik, pp. 427–428, and Bresnan, "A Realistic . . . Grammar," p. 59.

19. Richard Cureton provides an effective review of the major contributions to this debate in " 'he danced his did': An Analysis," *Journal of Linguistics* 16 (1980), 245–262. A late entry is James Paul Gee's "Anyone's Any: A View of Language and Poetry through an Analysis of 'anyone lived in a pretty how town,' " *Language and Style* 16:2 (1983), 123–137.

20. Otto Jespersen, *Essentials of English Grammar* (Birmingham: University of Alabama Press, 1964), p. 181; my emphasis.

21. I use the symbol "*" throughout this study to indicate that a sentence is unacceptable to most native speakers as a sample of standard English. I do not use it with material quoted from poetic texts.

I should also note that the full details of the distribution of *any* are considerably more complex than I have suggested here. I do not believe, however, that my simplification in any sense misrepresents the facts relevant to this particular literary application of them.

22. I am aware that my use of words such as *chosen, overlook,* and *transgress* implies a measure of consciousness on the part of the poet about the syntactic effects he has created. I return to this issue in chap. 5; see also Culler, pp. 117–118.

23. Their work has also been discussed by Cureton and by Tanya Reinhart, "Patterns, Intuitions, and the Sense of Nonsense," *PTL* 1 (1976), 85–103.

24. Samuel R. Levin, "Poetry and Grammaticalness," *Proceedings of the Ninth International Congress of Linguists,* ed. Horace G. Lunt (The Hague: Mouton, 1964). Rpt. in *Essays on the Language of Literature,* ed. Seymour Chatman and Samuel R. Levin (Boston: Houghton Mifflin, 1967), p. 226.

25. Ibid., p. 227.

26. James Peter Thorne, "Stylistics and Generative Grammars," *Journal of Linguistics* 1 (1965), 49–59; rpt. in *Linguistics and Literary Style,* ed. Donald C. Freeman (New York: Holt Rinehart & Winston, 1970), pp. 185–186. A reprise of essentially the same argument may be found in Thorne's later paper, "Generative Grammar and Stylistic Analysis," in *New Horizons in Linguistics,* ed. John Lyons (Harmondsworth: Penguin Books, 1970), pp. 185–197; rpt. in *Essays in Modern Stylistics,* ed. Donald C. Freeman (London and New York: Methuen, 1981), pp. 42–52. See also David A. Lee, " 'The Inheritors' and Transformational Generative Grammar," *Language and Style* IX (1976), 77–97.

27. Thorne, "Stylistics and Generative Grammars," p. 189. See also Reichert, pp. 26–27.

28. Thorne, "Stylistics and Generative Grammars," p. 187.

29. See for example Thorne, "Stylistics and Generative Grammars," p. 187, and Reinhart, pp. 91–93.

30. See Reinhart, p. 98, where her division of the poem, proposed on altogether independent grounds, is identical to that advanced here.

31. Ann M. Banfield, "Stylistic Transformations: A Study Based on the Syntax of 'Paradise Lost,'" Diss. University of Wisconsin 1973.

32. George L. Dillon, "Inversions and Deletions in English Poetry," *Language and Style* 8 (1975), 234–235.

33. Ibid., p. 221; my emphases.

34. Thus of cases very similar to some discussed immediately below as examples of poetic syntax violating completely the standard syntactic norms, Dillon remarks only that "this particular construction is probably ungrammatical, . . . but it is so common in Spenser that one must work out some strategy for it" (*Language Processing*, p. 36). Elsewhere he rephrases this same argument, asserting the need for stylists to devise "adjustment[s] for coping with ungrammatical texts" (p. 138).

35. Richard Cureton, "The Aesthetic Use of Syntax: Studies on the Syntax of the Poetry of E. E. Cummings," Diss. University of Illinois 1980, pp. 120–128, especially Strategies 5 and 6.

36. Citations from Shelley's works will be taken from Roger Ingpen and Walter E. Peck, eds., *The Complete Works of Percy Bysshe Shelley* (London and New York, 1927; rpt. New York: Gordian Press, 1965). Hereafter this edition will be cited as CWS; in referencing passages quoted, I shall include volume, page, and line numbers. Throughout this study, emphases, capitalizations, and punctuation will be those of the standard critical editions cited unless I note to the contrary.

37. Chomsky, "Conditions," p. 238.

38. See Bach, p. 212.

39. See S. Jay Keyser, "A Partial History of the Relative Clause in English," in *Papers in the History and Structure of English*, University of Massachusetts Occasional Papers in Linguistics, Vol. I, ed. Jane B. Grimshaw (Amherst: Graduate Linguistic Student Association, 1975), pp. 1–33; and Chomsky and Lasnik, p. 435.

40. George Miller and Noam Chomsky, "Finitary Models of Language Users," in *Handbook of Mathematical Psychology, II,* ed. R. D. Luce, R. R. Bush, and E. Galanter (New York: John Wiley & Sons, 1963), pp. 419–491. Further work on this topic is contained in Kuno.

41. Chomsky, *Aspects,* p. 127.

42. Banfield, pp. 134–135. This issue is also discussed by William P. Bivens III in "Parameters of Poetic Inversion in English," *Language and Style* XII (1979), 15–16.

43. Dillon, "Inversions and Deletions," p. 227; once again this point is recast in *Language Processing,* chap. 1.

44. Dillon discusses a number of similar cases from a reader-oriented standpoint in the early pages of *Language Processing.* His assertion that pragmatic and semantic criteria may often lead us never consciously to entertain certain structurally admissible interpretations seems to me plausible. He himself, however, notes several exceptions closely analogous to that

cited here (pp. 15, 20). My concern is, in any case, with such sentences' formal status with respect to syntactic competence rather than with the heuristic strategies we may or may not invoke to decode them (see chap. 5 of this study).

45. Carlos Baker, *Shelley's Major Poetry: The Fabric of a Vision* (1948; rpt. New York: Russell & Russell, 1961), p. 14.

46. Deborah Silverton Rosenfelt, "Keats and Shelley: A Comparative Study of their Ideas about Poetic Language and Some Patterns of Language Use in their Poetry," Diss. University of California, Los Angeles 1972, p. 127.

47. Fish, p. 259. See also, for example, his discussion of Freeman's paper on Keats's "To Autumn," pp. 263–266. Rather more surprisingly, we find Hirsch making a very similar accusation on p. 166 of *Validity in Interpretation*.

48. See Emmon Bach, "Comments on the Paper by Chomsky," in *Formal Syntax*, ed. P. Culicover, T. Wasow, and A. Akmajian (New York: Academic Press, 1977), pp. 133–156; and Janet Dean Fodor, "Parsing Strategies and Constraints on Transformations," *Linguistic Inquiry* 9 (1978), 427–473.

49. For an excellent survey of experimental evidence supporting this contention, see Herbert H. Clark and Eve V. Clark, *Psychology and Language: An Introduction to Psycholinguistics* (New York: Harcourt Brace Jovanovich, 1977), esp. pp. 45–84.

50. Dillon, "Inversions and Deletions," p. 229.

51. Thorne, "Stylistics and Generative Grammars," p. 191. See also Paul Ziff, "On Understanding 'Understanding Utterances,'" in *The Structure of Language: Readings in the Philosophy of Language*, ed. Jerry A. Fodor and Jerrold J. Katz (Englewood Cliffs, N.J.: Prentice-Hall, 1964), pp. 390–399.

52. John M. Lipski, "Poetic Deviance and Generative Grammar," *PTL* 2 (1977), 246; quoted in Cureton, "The Aesthetic Use of Syntax," p. 117.

53. Dillon, "Inversions and Deletions," p. 229; my emphasis.

54. *Language Processing*, p. xxx.

55. I do not want to imply that this feature was unique to Pope (a point I shall have to return to later in this study) nor that it was anything less than a much admired virtue of his style in the eyes of most of his contemporaries; see Donald Davie [*Articulate Energy* (London: Routledge & Kegan Paul, 1955), p. 60] who claims that for Augustan poets generally "'strength' . . . is close and compact syntax, neither more nor less."

56. Citations from Pope's works will be taken from John Butt, ed., *The Poems of Alexander Pope* (London: Methuen, 1963), hereafter PAP; in referencing passages, I shall include the name of the work, unless that has been specified elsewhere in the immediate context, and the relevant page and line numbers.

57. This hypothesis itself would constitute an interesting methodological principle with obvious links to common-sense reader strategies for processing poetic material. However, it lies beyond the immediate scope of this discussion.

58. See Ray Jackendoff, "Gapping and Related Rules," *Linguistic In-*

quiry 2 (1971), 21–35; Susumu Kuno, "Gapping: A Functional Analysis," *Linguistic Inquiry* 7:2 (1976), 300–318; John R. Ross, *Constraints,* and "Gapping and the Order of Constituents," in *Progress in Linguistics,* ed. M. Bierwisch and K. E. Heidolph (The Hague: Mouton, 1970); and Justine T. Stillings, "The Formulation of Gapping in English as Evidence for Variable Types in Syntactic Transformations," *Linguistic Analysis* 1 (1975), 247–273.

59. I am aware that, given the versatility of transformational grammars and the range of human ingenuity, innumerable other hypotheses may be cobbled up on demand. I am, however, more interested here in the question of how a stylist chooses between competing theories than in the theories themselves. In any case, "[s]cience *must* proceed not by experimentally testing all imaginable theories . . . but by rejecting all but a very small number of theories as *a priori* too implausible to be worth testing" (Putnam, p. 25).

60. For a specification of these rather complex restrictions, see the sources cited in note 58.

61. See Barbara Abbott, "Right Node Raising as a Test for Constituenthood," *Linguistic Inquiry* 7 (1976), 639–642; Alexander Grosu, "A Note on Subject Raising to Object and Right Node Raising," *Linguistic Inquiry* 7 (1976), 642–645; Jorge Hankamer, "Constraints on Deletion in Syntax," Diss. Yale University 1971; and Richard A. Hudson, "Conjunction Reduction, Gapping and Right-Node Raising," *Language* 52 (1976), 535–562.

62. A chance remark in Dillon's constantly stimulating paper suggests yet a third possible approach. In categorizing deletion patterns common in English poetic texts, Dillon simply notes that "where [a] deleted element would normally be pronominal in Modern English, D.O.'s [direct objects] are deleted to the right" ("Inversions and Deletions," p. 221). His description prompts us to consider the possibility of a *Rightward Pronoun Drop* rule as another means of generating the structures we have encountered in Pope's poetry. Such a rule might have several rather attractive features. Limiting deletion to pronominal direct objects in conjoined sentences would make this rule less sweeping than either rightward Right Node Raising or Conjunct Scrambling; and the proposed rule bears an intriguing resemblance to a more general rule of anaphoric pronoun deletion often attributed to Old and Middle English syntax [see F. Th. Visser, *An Historical Syntax of the English Language* (Leiden: E. J. Brill, 1963), p. 525]. Alas, this solution too runs afoul of a specific construction in the Pope corpus, this time a famous couplet from "The Rape of the Lock": "Here Thou, Great *Anna!* whom three Realms obey,/ Dost sometimes Counsel take—and sometimes *Tea."* (PAP, 227: 7–8). Here we find no overt verb in the second conjunct, but by definition a Rightward Pronoun Drop rule cannot be held responsible for the deletion of the verb *take.* We shall thus be forced back, in this particular case, either on rightward Right Node Raising or on leftward Right Node Raising combined with Conjunct Scrambling, if we wish to explain the deletion that has clearly occurred.

63. For brevity's sake I omitted numerous examples paralleling that

cited from "The Epistle to Dr. Arbuthnot"; some interesting cases may also be found in Dillon, "Inversions and Deletions."

64. Noam Chomsky, *Current Issues in Linguistic Theory* (The Hague: Mouton, 1964), chap. 2.

65. Jerry A. Fodor, Thomas G. Bever, and Merrill F. Garrett, *The Psychology of Language* (New York: McGraw-Hill, 1974), p. 85. For a more general discussion of what makes scientific hypotheses "simple," desirable, or "plausible" in this sense, see Hilary Putnam, *Mathematics, Matter and Method: Philosophical Papers, Volume 1* (Cambridge: Cambridge University Press, 1975), pp. 351–354.

66. See, for example, Ohmann's work on Shaw cited in chap. 1.

67. Harold Whitehall, "From Linguistics to Criticism," *Kenyon Review* XIII (1951), 713; cited in Freeman, *Linguistics and Literary Style*, p. 3.

3. The Aesthetic Dimension

1. Ahmad K. Ardat, "The Prose Style of Selected Works by Ernest Hemingway, Sherwood Anderson and Gertrude Stein," *Style* 14 (1980), 3. (The journal *Style* specializes in such studies and frequently reviews the whole field of stylistic statistics.)

2. Fish, p. 74.

3. Compare Leech and Short, pp. 14 and 42–48.

4. Citations of Dryden's work refer to H. T. Swedenberg, ed., *The Works of John Dryden* (Berkeley and Los Angeles: University of California Press, 1956), hereafter WJD; references list volume, page, and line numbers as well as the title of the poem quoted from, wherever this information is not already given in the text.

5. It may seem that I assume too easily here and elsewhere in this study that reading poetry involves rather mechanical "real time," left-to-right analysis. I would not seek to deny the charge outright. Indeed, that some carefully qualified concept of "the linearity of text" is indispensable in literary stylistics is strongly argued by Leech and Short (pp. 210–212) who also cite Fish in the same vein. But we shall have cause to reexamine the whole issue of "the reader" from a rather different perspective in chap. 5.

6. Here and elsewhere in this discussion I shall use the terms "distance" and "delay" interchangeably. As will become clear when I analyze their formal status as stylistic concepts later in the chapter, these terms effectively constitute a matched pair, related respectively to our experience of poetry along spatial and temporal dimensions.

7. See Clark and Clark, pp. 66–68. Dillon also discusses at some length cases of that kind in literary contexts in *Language Processing*, p. 24. He attributes the garden-path metaphor to Henry Fowler.

8. Thus, for example, linguistic theory has seldom found that it needed to define or to measure the "distance" between syntactic constituents. The obvious exception proving this generalization—Peter Rosenbaum's reliance on distance calculations as part of his "erasure principle" governing comple-

ment sentence interpretation [*The Grammar of English Predicate Complement Constructions* (Cambridge: MIT Press, 1967), p. 6]—has been obviated by subsequent developments in syntactic theory itself.

9. Citations of Byron's works refer to Frederick Page, ed., *Byron: Poetical Works,* Oxford Standard Authors edn., corr. John Jump (London: Oxford University Press, 1970), hereafter BPW; references list the relevant work's title, where necessary, and page and line numbers.

10. Stylistic delay caused by syntactic manipulation (often mistermed "syntactic tension," as I shall explain below) has of course already received extensive discussion in the literature. Donald Davie finds an excellent example in T. S. Eliot's "Gerontion" (Davie, pp. 88–89). A parallel case discovered in Dylan Thomas' poetry by Donald Freeman was already outlined in the opening pages of chapter 1. Both Richard Cureton ("The Aesthetic Use of Syntax," pp. 175 ff.) and Irene Fairley ["Syntactic Deviation and Cohesion," *Language and Style* VI:3 (1973), 220] offer parallel examples drawn from the works of E. E. Cummings. In the field of prose style analysis, meanwhile, George Dillon cites an excellent discussion by Jane Tompkins of a passage from Henry James' "The Beast in the Jungle" (*Language Processing,* p. 135); and Leech and Short devote major sections of chap. 7 of their book to this same topic.

I shall take issue with some of the specific assumptions and indeed conclusions of these analyses in the pages that follow. Nonetheless, I am fully aware of the groundwork that has been so expertly laid in this particular area.

11. Cureton, "The Aesthetic Use of Syntax," p. 27 (my emphasis); see also his chap. 1 (passim).

12. Gwendolyn Brooks, *The World of Gwendolyn Brooks* (New York: Harper & Row, 1959).

13. Susanne Langer, *Philosophy in a New Key: A Study in the Symbolism of Reason, Rite, and Art* (Cambridge: Harvard University Press, 1942), pp. 260–261; cited in Davie, p. 18.

14. As used by Leech and Short, pp. 226 ff.

15. See for example Cureton, "The Aesthetic Use of Syntax"; Davie, pp. 85–91; Donald C. Freeman, "Keats's 'To Autumn': Poetry as Process and Pattern," *Language and Style* XI (1978), 3–17; Jakobson; Kiparsky; Samuel R. Levin, *Linguistic Structures in Poetry* (The Hague: Mouton, 1962); and R. G. Peterson, "Critical Calculations: Measure and Symmetry in Literature," *PMLA* 91 (1976), 367–375.

16. Peter Quennell, *Byron: A Self-Portrait* (New York: Humanities Press, 1967), II, p. 516.

17. That this equation is in fact proposed without proper qualification may be seen if one considers the unstated implications of the following sentence from no less an authority than *The Norton Anthology of English Literature:* "Within [the] two lines [of the heroic couplet] it was possible to attain certain rhetorical or witty effects by the use of parallelism, balance, or antithesis within the couplet as a whole or the individual line" (I, p. 1730).

One cannot blame the student who infers from this remark that, *outside* the heroic couplet mode, such effects as "parallelism, balance, and antithesis" have been, and indeed still may be, altogether impossible.

18. Baker, p. 23. The critical views expressed in this paragraph accord with, and have been considerably influenced by, the work of Desmond King-Hele [*Shelley: His Thought and Work* (Teaneck, N.J.: Fairleigh Dickinson University Press, 1971), esp. pp. 42 ff.]; Melvin T. Solve [*Shelley: His Theory of Poetry* (Chicago: University of Chicago Press, 1927), esp. pp. 36 ff.]; and Floyd H. Stovall [*Desire and Restraint in Shelley* (Durham, N.C.: Duke University Press, 1931), esp. pp. 140–141].

19. Baker, p. 37 (my emphasis).

20. Earl Miner, *Dryden's Poetry* (Bloomington and London: Indiana University Press, 1967), p. 146.

21. The term is T. S. Eliot's [*The Use of Poetry and the Use of Criticism* (Cambridge: Harvard University Press, 1933), p. 83]; see also Solve, pp. 149 ff.

22. I do not have space here to address the possibility that triadic structures may represent "a conventional means to elevation" of style regardless of the context in which they appear, a claim advanced by K. G. Hamilton [*John Dryden and the Poetry of Statement* (Lansing: Michigan State University Press, 1969), p. 142] and by Winston Weathers ["The Rhetoric of the Series," in *Teaching Freshman Composition,* ed. Gary Tate and Edward P. J. Corbett (New York: Oxford University Press, 1967), pp. 313–319].

23. I refer throughout to E. H. Coleridge's standard edition, *The Complete Poetical Works of Samuel Taylor Coleridge* (Oxford: The Clarendon Press, 1912), hereafter CPW. As usual, I list each work's title, and the relevant volume, page, and line references, wherever necessary, immediately following each quotation.

24. The name is due to John R. Ross (unpublished mimeo notes); but see also S. Jay Keyser, rev. of *Adverbial Positions in English,* by Sven Jacobson, *Language* 44 (1968), 357–373; and Justine T. Stillings, "Sentence Raising" (Bloomington: Indiana University Linguistics Club, 1975).

25. The dangers inherent in accepting such self-assessments in the case of this particular poet have been well documented in Norman Fruman's *Coleridge: The Damaged Archangel* (New York: George Braziller, 1971). The present discussion will represent yet another reason for crediting Fruman's allegation that Coleridge's remarkable critical powers were exceeded only by his acute feelings of personal insecurity.

26. "O!" wrote Coleridge in his notebooks, "it is the relation of facts— not the facts, friend!" [*Anima Poetae: From the Unpublished Note-books of Samuel Taylor Coleridge,* ed. Ernest Hartley Coleridge (London, 1895; rpt. Pennsylvania: The Folcroft Press, 1969), p. 148] The same emphasis on "relation" (and indeed even that word itself) reappears in Coleridge's definition of poetic genius elsewhere in the notebooks (p. 233).

For other references to the dell as a symbol, see "Pantisocracy" (CPW I, 68–69) and "To a Young Ass" (CPW I, 74–76, esp. line 27). I discuss the general function of this symbol in Coleridge's poetry and in his life in chap. 2 of my dissertation, "A Linguistic Approach to the Style of the English Early Romantic Poets," Diss. University of Massachusetts 1977.

27. Jonathan Culler discusses at some length in chap. 3 of his *Structuralist Poetics* this problem with Jakobsonian analysis, the nagging feeling one has that "with a little inventiveness, symmetries of all kinds can be discovered" in any work (p. 58). He subsequently defends stylists' methods from their more violent detractors, however, along lines similar to those developed in the rest of this paragraph.

28. For another paper that exploits broad structural congruencies of this kind, see S. Jay Keyser, "Wallace Stevens: Form and Meaning in Four Poems," *College English* 37 (1976), 63–101.

29. *Collected Letters of Samuel Taylor Coleridge,* ed. Earl Leslie Griggs (Oxford: The Clarendon Press, 1956), p. 381.

30. Is it too fanciful to see again here the same pun on *round* and *around* that we noted before in our discussion of "Reflections . . ."?

31. "A Linguistic Approach," pp. 18–19 and 55–71.

32. One of many fascinating footnotes in CPW offers admittedly circumstantial evidence that an earlier version of this line may in fact have read not "honey-dew" but "fields of dew" (CPW I, 298: fn. 2). Coleridge's subsequent revision, if this was indeed the case, permitted him, as we shall shortly see, to create a syntactic pattern which would have been impossible with *dew* as modifier rather than as head of its construction.

33. The term "prominent" as it appears here and in the discussions that follow represents a useful shorthand means for taking into account a number of complex and inherently relativistic judgments that readers make about different aspects of a literary text. Chap. 2 of Leech and Short's study of prose style includes an excellent discussion of this word and of allied terms such as "foregrounding," "frequency," and "deviance."

34. My reference to Verb Final here is occasioned by the fact that, for some reason that I do not fully understand, I cannot read the fourth clause of this passage as a topicalized sentence with the first preverbal NP as its object. Verb Final must therefore be invoked to give the surface Subject-Object-Verb order that I instinctively assign it.

35. Cureton, "The Aesthetic Use of Syntax," pp. 147 ff.

36. Quotations from *The Ruined Cottage* use the text printed in Jonathan Wordsworth's *The Music of Humanity* (New York and Evanston, Ill.: Harper & Row, 1969), hereafter TMH; line numbers alone will be used to identify the passages quoted, all of which come from Part I of the poem.

37. As defined in Ross, *Constraints,* example 5.46.

38. Unable to keep from meddling with his own best work, Wordsworth destroyed many of the beauties of the opening lines of this poem when revising them for inclusion in Book I of *The Excursion* [see Jonathan Wordsworth's comments in TMH; and Timothy R. Austin, "Stylistic Evolution in Wordsworth's Poetry: Evidence from Emendations," *Language and Style* 12 (1979), 176–187]. This was certainly true of the "dappled syntax" of the pas-

sage discussed here. In the 1814 text, Wordsworth wrote mundanely of "[a] surface dappled o'er with shadows flung/From brooding clouds" (lines 5–6). The availability of this clearly inferior textual variant for comparison renders particularly vivid, I think, the role that syntax can play in establishing coherence for a passage as a whole.

4. The Task of Interpretation

1. Smith, p. 160.

2. Fish, p. 78.

3. Irene Fairley, "Experimental Approaches to Language in Literature: Reader Responses to Poems," *Style* 13:4 (1979), 335.

4. Culler, p. 118.

5. See Freeman, "Literature as Property"; Leech and Short, p. 13; and Muffy E. A. Siegel, " 'The Original Crime': John Berryman's Iconic Grammar," *Poetics Today* 2:1a (1980), p. 170.

6. Smith, p. 170.

7. Fish, p. 82.

8. Roger Fowler, "Language and the Reader: Shakespeare's Sonnet 73," in *Style and Structure in Literature: Essays in the New Stylistics,* ed. Roger Fowler (Ithaca, N.Y.: Cornell University Press, 1975), pp. 120, 122 (my emphasis). Compare with this the almost precisely parallel statement of intent in Leech and Short, pp. 2–5.

9. E. L. Epstein, "The Self-Reflexive Artefact: The Function of Mimesis in an Approach to a Theory of Value for Literature," in *Style and Structure in Literature: Essays in the New Stylistics,* ed. Roger Fowler (Ithaca, N.Y.: Cornell University Press, 1975), p. 41.

10. Ibid., p. 40; my emphasis.

11. Ibid., p. 75. I dispute the specifically *evaluative* application of Epstein's discoveries in chap. 5 of this study.

12. Fish, p. 76.

13. Since Fish also, of course, attributes to transformational grammarians beliefs in the absolute truth of their *grammatical* model that I cannot myself find in my reading of those authors, this part of his attack on *stylistics* was perhaps predictable.

14. Hirsch, p. 170; see also Armstrong, p. 342.

15. Fowler, *Style and Structure,* p. 8.

16. Freeman, "The Strategy of Fusion," p. 39.

17. Ibid., p. 20.

18. It is interesting in this light that Smith stages a brief but intense attack on *historical* criticism in terms that very much resemble those already cited from her critique of stylistics: "this sort of interpretation is absurd . . . because the invocation of particulars of this kind . . . *have no greater claim to constituting the 'meaning' of the poem* than an interpretation that infers from it" a meaning "quite independent" of its historical origins (p. 35; emphases my own). I could not agree more that critical insight

represents the only "greater claim" to legitimacy for any statement about a text.

19. Smith, pp. 170–171.

20. "Experimental Approaches," p. 335.

21. Smith, p. 170; my emphasis.

22. "There is a cyclic motion whereby linguistic observation stimulates or modifies literary insight, and whereby literary insight in its turn stimulates further linguistic observation. This motion is something like the cycle of theory formulation and theory testing which underlies scientific method" (Leech and Short, p. 13, who also cite Leo Spitzer in the same vein). Compare Armstrong, pp. 341–343; and Richard Rorty, *Philosophy and the Mirror of Nature* (Princeton, N.J.: Princeton University Press, 1979), chap. VII.

23. "Constraints," pp. 324–330.

24. See Ross, *Constraints*, example 4.20; and George M. Horn, "The Noun Phrase Constraint," Diss. University of Massachusetts 1974.

25. A. Clutton-Brock, *Shelley: The Man and the Poet* (New York: G. P. Putnam's Sons, 1909), p. 144.

26. Leech and Short, p. 42.

27. As I have already stressed (perhaps almost too insistently), this correspondence is entirely local and temporary. I find it wholly refreshing, therefore, that George Dillon, discussing confusing cases of apposition in the works of Wallace Stevens and William Faulkner, should see in those constructions—"sentences that are ill-formed any way you parse them"—not a reflection of human imperfections but an attempt by those particular authors "to achieve the romantic . . . apprehension of a wholeness beyond all distinctions" (*Language Processing*, p. 113).

28. Smith, pp. 163–164.

29. Great care must be exercised, however, in reading such material. The word "iconic" has frequently been used in ways very different from that intended here. In the title of Freeman's "Iconic Syntax in Poetry: A Note on Blake's 'Ah! Sun-Flower' " [in *U/Mass Occasional Papers in Linguistics II*, ed. Justine T. Stillings (Amherst: Graduate Linguistic Student Association, University of Massachusetts, 1976), pp. 51–57], "iconic" is employed to characterize a group of stylistic effects that I would want instead to term *mimetic*. By the same token, not all of Cureton's "iconic" effects as listed in "The Aesthetic Use of Syntax" would in fact be so classified under my own guidelines. It will assuredly take time for usage of these technical terms to achieve any real stability—time whose passing this chapter is designed to hasten.

30. My text for the early draft of this poem is taken from Griggs' *Collected Letters*, Vol. I, pp. 334–336. A letter draft to Lloyd, cited in CPW I, 178 (fn.), does not appear in Griggs' collection. Though that version represents still a third variant over the Southey letter and the published text, the alternate readings it introduces do not in any way affect the point I make here about syntactic iconicity.

31. Not, of course, that I wish to denigrate critical claims that make appeal to readers' intuitions. I myself described Shelley's syntactic choices

in "Adonais" as "intuitively apt" earlier in this chapter. That does not prevent me from enjoying those rare cases where more tangible evidence is available to support my contentions.

32. Leech and Short note a similar prose example from Lyly's *Euphues:* "the repetition in parallel of examples from different spheres of experience . . . enforces the generality of a didactic principle which is otherwise seen to be particular" (p. 17).

33. Here and in the pages that follow, I elaborate on ideas first advanced in studies such as Jakobson; Kiparsky; and Levin, *Linguistic Structures in Poetry.* My discussion constitutes, in fact, a series of steps towards a yet more sophisticated sense of *how* precisely "the repetition of 'linguistic sames' " pinpointed by those theorists as central to poetic syntax "can come to have meaning" in complex and elaborate poetic contexts (Siegel, p. 166).

34. Dillon, "Inversions and Deletions," passim.

35. See Culler, p. 119.

36. That readers consider such a possibility is also argued by Leech and Short, pp. 142–143.

37. Mark van Doren, *John Dryden: A Study of his Poetry* (New York: Henry Holt, 1946), p. 69.

38. George Williamson, "The Rhetorical Pattern of Neo-Classical Wit," *Modern Philology* 33 (1935), 55.

39. *John Dryden and the Poetry of Statement,* p. 46.

40. Williamson, p. 81.

41. Hamilton, p. 89.

42. Paul Ramsey, *The Art of John Dryden* (Lexington: University of Kentucky Press, 1969), p. 72.

43. Hamilton, chap. 2; Ramsey, chap. 6.

5. Conclusions Theoretical and Pedagogical

1. As I have noted elsewhere, Dillon's *Language Processing* represents the state of the art in the field of language processing theory that parallels stylistics as I define it.

2. W. Daniel Wilson, "Readers in Texts," *PMLA* 96 (1981), 848, 856. I refer the reader to this article for a most informative discussion of much of the material alluded to here. Additional commentary may be found in Jane P. Tompkins, ed., *Reader-Response Criticism: From Formalism to Post-Structuralism* (Baltimore: The Johns Hopkins University Press, 1980).

3. Wilson, p. 856.

4. Ibid.

5. It might seem folly to introduce here yet another construct for fellow theorists to attack, rename, dissect, or befriend. My discussion throughout the preceding pages has, however, created that construct already by presupposing it. To evade the tasks of defining it clearly and explaining the role it plays within my stylistic theory would merely invite misunderstanding and misrepresentation.

6. It also parallels Jonathan Culler's reliance on the notion of an "ideal reader" in his development of a theory of *literary* competence (Culler, p. 124).

7. Armstrong, p. 343.

8. Ibid., p. 347.

9. This idea was first suggested to me, in fact, by a member of the audience at a session of the 1979 Summer Meeting of the Linguistic Society of America in Salzburg, Austria.

10. My phrasing as I spelt out my conclusions in this paragraph—"*A* would be compatible with *B*," "*C* does not absolutely conflict with *D*"—will be familiar enough to linguists. In my theory of syntactic stylistics, as in linguistic theory itself, the primacy of the internal consistency of the theory remains absolute. I am delighted, that is, to find that certain classroom data seem consistent with my theoretical hypothesis in one particular case. Even were closer examination to prove those data worthless, however, I would not renounce the technical analysis with which they apparently correlate. As Jonathan Culler notes: "[C]laims about literary [and stylistic] competence are not to be verified by surveys of readers' reactions to poems but by readers' assent to the . . . efficacy of [the resulting] explanatory hypotheses" (Culler, pp. 125–126).

11. "Stylistic Evolution," pp. 180–187.

Bibliography

Abbott, Barbara. "Right Node Raising as a Test for Constituenthood." *Linguistic Inquiry* 7 (1976), 639–642.

Akmajian, Adrian and Frank Heny. *An Introduction to the Principles of Transformational Syntax*. Cambridge and London: MIT Press, 1975.

Ardat, Ahmad K. "The Prose Style of Selected Works by Ernest Hemingway, Sherwood Anderson and Gertrude Stein." *Style* 14 (1980), 1–21.

Armstrong, Paul B. "The Conflict of Interpretations and the Limits of Pluralism." *PMLA* 98 (1983), 341–352.

Austin, Timothy R. "A Linguistic Approach to the Style of the English Early Romantic Poets." Diss. University of Massachusetts 1977.

——. "Stylistic Evolution in Wordsworth's Poetry: Evidence from Emendations." *Language and Style* 12 (1979), 176–187.

——. "Constraints on Syntactic Rules and the Style of Shelley's 'Adonais': An Exercise in Stylistic Criticism." *PTL* 4 (1979), 315–343. Rpt. in *Essays in Modern Stylistics*. Ed. Donald C. Freeman. London and New York: Methuen, 1981, pp. 138–165.

——. "Prolegomenon to a Theory of Comparative Poetic Syntax." *Language and Style* 16 (1983), 433–455.

Bach, Emmon. *Syntactic Theory*. New York: Holt Rinehart & Winston, 1974.

——. "Comments on the Paper by Chomsky." In *Formal Syntax*. Ed. P. Culicover, T. Wasow, and A. Akmajian. New York: Academic Press, 1977, pp. 133–156.

——, and George M. Horn. "Remarks on 'Conditions on Transformations.'" *Linguistic Inquiry* 7:2 (1976), 265–299.

Baker, Carlos. *Shelley's Major Poetry: The Fabric of a Vision.* 1948; rpt. New York: Russell & Russell, 1961.

Banfield, Ann M. "Stylistic Transformations: A Study Based on the Syntax of 'Paradise Lost.'" Diss. University of Wisconsin 1973.

Bever, Thomas G. See Fodor, Jerry A., Thomas G. Bever, and Merrill F. Garrett.

Bivens, William P., III. "Parameters of Poetic Inversion in English." *Language and Style* XII (1979), 13–25.

Bloomfield, Leonard. *Language*. London: George Allen & Unwin, 1935.

Bresnan, Joan W. "On Complementizers: Toward a Syntactic Theory of Complement Types." *Foundations of Language* 6 (1970), 297–321.

——. "A Realistic Transformational Grammar." In *Linguistic Theory and Psychological Reality*. Ed. Morris Halle, Joan Bresnan, and George A. Miller. Cambridge and London: MIT Press, 1978, pp. 1–59.

Brooks, Gwendolyn. *The World of Gwendolyn Brooks*. New York: Harper & Row, 1959.

Butt, John, ed. *The Poems of Alexander Pope*. London: Methuen, 1963.

Byron, George Gordon, Lord. See Page, Frederick, ed.

Chatman, Seymour. "Milton's Participial Style." *PMLA* 83 (1968), 1386–1399.

——. *The Later Style of Henry James*. Oxford: Blackwells Press, 1972.

——, and Samuel R. Levin, eds. *Essays on the Language of Literature*. Boston: Houghton Mifflin, 1967.

157

Chomsky, Noam. See Miller, George and Noam Chomsky.
————. *Syntactic Structures.* The Hague: Mouton, 1957.
————. *Current Issues in Linguistic Theory.* The Hague: Mouton, 1964.
————. *Aspects of the Theory of Syntax.* Cambridge: MIT Press, 1965.
————. *Language and Mind.* New York: Harcourt Brace Jovanovich, 1972.
————. "Some Empirical Issues in the Theory of Transformational Grammar." In *Goals of Linguistic Theory.* Ed. Stanley Peters. Englewood Cliffs, N.J.: Prentice-Hall, 1972, pp. 63–130.
————. "Conditions on Transformations." In *A Festschrift for Morris Halle.* Ed. Stephen R. Anderson and Paul Kiparsky. New York: Holt Rinehart & Winston, 1973, pp. 232–286.
————. *Reflections on Language.* New York: Pantheon Books, 1975.
————, and Howard Lasnik. "Filters and Control." *Linguistic Inquiry* 8 (1977), 425–504.
Clark, Eve V. See Clark, Herbert H. and Eve V. Clark.
Clark, Herbert H. and Eve V. Clark. *Psychology and Language: An Introduction to Psycholinguistics.* New York: Harcourt Brace Jovanovich, 1977.
Clutton-Brock, A. *Shelley: The Man and the Poet.* New York: G. P. Putnam's Sons, 1909.
Coleridge, Ernest Hartley, ed. *Anima Poetae: From the Unpublished Notebooks of Samuel Taylor Coleridge.* London, 1895; rpt. Pennsylvania: The Folcroft Press, 1969.
————, ed. *The Complete Poetical Works of Samuel Taylor Coleridge.* Oxford: The Clarendon Press, 1912.
Coleridge, Samuel Taylor. See Coleridge, Ernest Hartley, ed., and Griggs, Earl Leslie, ed.
Culler, Jonathan. *Structuralist Poetics.* London and Ithaca, N.Y.: Routledge & Kegan Paul and Cornell University Press, 1975.
Cureton, Richard D. "The Aesthetic Use of Syntax: Studies on the Syntax of the Poetry of E. E. Cummings." Diss. University of Illinois 1980.
————. " 'he danced his did': An Analysis." *Journal of Linguistics* 16 (1980), 245–262.
Davie, Donald. *Articulate Energy.* London: Routledge & Kegan Paul, 1955.
Derrida, Jacques. "Signature Event Context." *Glyph* 1 (1977), 172–197.
————. "Limited Inc.: a b c . . ." *Glyph* 2 (1978), 162–254.
Dillon, George L. "Inversions and Deletions in English Poetry." *Language and Style* 8 (1975), 220–237.
————. *Language Processing and the Reading of Literature: Toward a Model of Comprehension.* Bloomington and London: Indiana University Press, 1978.
Dryden, John. See Swedenberg, H. T., ed.
Eliot, T. S. *The Use of Poetry and the Use of Criticism.* Cambridge: Harvard University Press, 1933.
Emonds, Joseph. *A Transformational Approach to English Syntax.* New York: Academic Press, 1976.
Epstein, E. L. "The Self-Reflexive Artefact: The Function of Mimesis in an Approach to a Theory of Value for Literature." In *Style and Structure in Literature: Essays in the New Stylistics.* Ed. Roger Fowler. Ithaca, N.Y.: Cornell University Press, 1975, pp. 40–78.

Fairley, Irene R. "Syntactic Deviation and Cohesion." *Language and Style* VI:3 (1973), 216–229. Rpt. in *Essays in Modern Stylistics*. Ed. Donald C. Freeman. London and New York: Methuen, 1981, pp. 123–137.

———. "Experimental Approaches to Language in Literature: Reader Responses to Poems." *Style* 13:4 (1979), 335–364.

Fish, Stanley. *Is There A Text In This Class?* Cambridge and London: Harvard University Press, 1980.

Fodor, Janet Dean. "Parsing Strategies and Constraints on Transformations." *Linguistic Inquiry* 9 (1978), 427–473.

Fodor, Jerry A., Thomas G. Bever, and Merrill F. Garrett. *The Psychology of Language*. New York: McGraw-Hill, 1974.

Fowler, Roger, ed. *Style and Structure in Literature: Essays in the New Stylistics*. Ithaca, N.Y.: Cornell University Press, 1975.

———. "Language and the Reader: Shakespeare's Sonnet 73." In *Style and Structure in Literature: Essays in the New Stylistics*. Ed. Roger Fowler. Ithaca, N.Y.: Cornell University Press, 1975, pp. 79–122.

Freeman, Donald C., ed. *Linguistics and Literary Style*. New York: Holt Rinehart & Winston, 1970.

———. "The Strategy of Fusion: Dylan Thomas's Syntax." In *Style and Structure in Literature: Essays in the New Stylistics*. Ed. Roger Fowler. Ithaca, N.Y.: Cornell University Press, 1975, pp. 19–39.

———. "Iconic Syntax in Poetry: A Note on Blake's 'Ah! Sun-Flower.'" In *U/Mass Occasional Papers in Linguistics II*. Ed. Justine T. Stillings. Amherst: Graduate Linguistic Student Association, University of Massachusetts, 1976, pp. 51–57.

———. "Keats's 'To Autumn': Poetry as Process and Pattern." *Language and Style* XI (1978), 3–17. Rpt. in *Essays in Modern Stylistics*. Ed. Donald C. Freeman. London and New York: Methuen, 1981, pp. 83–99.

———. "Literature as Property: A Review Article." *Language and Style* 13:2 (1980), 156–173.

———, ed. *Essays in Modern Stylistics*. London and New York: Methuen, 1981.

Fruman, Norman. *Coleridge: The Damaged Archangel*. New York: George Braziller, 1971.

Garrett, Merrill F. See Fodor, Jerry A., Thomas G. Bever, and Merrill F. Garrett.

Gee, James Paul. "Anyone's Any: A View of Language and Poetry Through an Analysis of 'anyone lived in a pretty how town.'" *Language and Style* 16:2 (1983), 123–137.

Graff, Gerald. *Literature Against Itself*. Chicago and London: University of Chicago Press, 1979.

Griggs, Earl Leslie, ed. *Collected Letters of Samuel Taylor Coleridge*. Oxford: The Clarendon Press, 1956.

Grosu, Alexander. "A Note on Subject Raising to Object and Right Node Raising." *Linguistic Inquiry* 7 (1976), 642–645.

Halle, Morris and S. Jay Keyser. *English Stress: Its Form, Its Growth, and Its Role in Verse*. New York: Harper & Row, 1971.

Halliday, M. A. K. "Descriptive Linguistics in Literary Studies." In *English Studies Today*. Ed. G. I. Duthie. Edinburgh: Edinburgh University Press, 1964. Rpt. in *Linguistics and Literary Style*. Ed. Donald C. Freeman. New York: Holt Rinehart & Winston, 1970, pp. 57–72.

Hamilton, K. G. *John Dryden and the Poetry of Statement.* Lansing: Michigan State University Press, 1969.

Hankamer, Jorge. "Constraints on Deletion in Syntax." Diss. Yale University 1971.

Heny, Frank. See Akmajian, Adrian and Frank Heny.

Hirsch, E. D. *Validity in Interpretation.* New Haven and London: Yale University Press, 1967.

———. *The Aims of Interpretation.* Chicago: University of Chicago Press, 1976.

Horn, George M. See Bach, Emmon and George M. Horn.

———. "The Noun Phrase Constraint." Diss. University of Massachusetts 1974.

Hudson, Richard A. "Conjunction Reduction, Gapping and Right-Node Raising." *Language* 52 (1976), 535–562.

Ingpen, Roger and Walter E. Peck, eds. *The Complete Works of Percy Bysshe Shelley.* London and New York, 1927; rpt. New York: Gordian Press, 1965.

Jackendoff, Ray. "Gapping and Related Rules." *Linguistic Inquiry* 2 (1971), 21–35.

———. *Semantic Interpretation in Generative Grammar.* Cambridge and London: MIT Press, 1972.

———. "Morphological and Semantic Regularities in the Lexicon." *Language* 51 (1975), 639–671.

Jakobson, Roman. "Linguistics and Poetics." In *Style in Language.* Ed. Thomas A. Sebeok. Cambridge: MIT Press, 1960, pp. 350–377. Rpt. in *Essays on the Language of Literature.* Ed. Seymour Chatman and Samuel R. Levin. Boston: Houghton Mifflin, 1967, pp. 296–322.

Jespersen, Otto. *Essentials of English Grammar.* Birmingham: University of Alabama Press, 1964.

Jump, John, ed. See Page, Frederick, ed.

Kermode, Frank. *The Sense of an Ending.* New York: Oxford University Press, 1967.

Keyser, S. Jay. See Halle, Morris and S. Jay Keyser.

———. Rev. of *Adverbial Positions in English*, by Sven Jacobson. *Language* 44 (1968), 357–373.

———. "A Partial History of the Relative Clause in English." In *Papers in the History and Structure of English.* University of Massachusetts Occasional Papers in Linguistics, Vol. I. Ed. Jane B. Grimshaw. Amherst: Graduate Linguistic Student Association, 1975, pp. 1–33.

———. "Wallace Stevens: Form and Meaning in Four Poems." *College English* 37 (1976), 63–101. Rpt. in *Essays in Modern Stylistics.* Ed. Donald C. Freeman. London and New York: Methuen, 1981, pp. 100–122.

King-Hele, Desmond. *Shelley: His Thought and Work.* Teaneck, N.J.: Fairleigh Dickinson University Press, 1971.

Kiparsky, Paul. "The Role of Linguistics in a Theory of Poetry." *Daedalus* 102 (1973), 231–244. Rpt. in *Essays in Modern Stylistics.* Ed. Donald C. Freeman. London and New York: Methuen, 1981, pp. 9–23.

Kuno, Susumu. "The Position of Relative Clauses and Conjunctions." *Linguistic Inquiry* 5:1 (1974), 117–136.

———. "Gapping: A Functional Analysis." *Linguistic Inquiry* 7:2 (1976), 300–318.

Langer, Susanne. *Philosophy in a New Key: A Study in the Symbolism of Reason, Rite, and Art.* Cambridge: Harvard University Press, 1942.

Lasnik, Howard. See Chomsky, Noam and Howard Lasnik.

Lee, David A. " 'The Inheritors' and Transformational Generative Grammar." *Language and Style* IX (1976), 77–97.

Leech, Geoffrey N. and Michael H. Short. *Style in Fiction: A Linguistic Introduction to English Fictional Prose.* London and New York: Longman, 1981.

Levin, Samuel R. See Chatman, Seymour and Samuel R. Levin.

———. *Linguistic Structures in Poetry.* The Hague: Mouton, 1962.

———. "Poetry and Grammaticalness." *Proceedings of the Ninth International Congress of Linguists.* Ed. Horace G. Lunt. The Hague: Mouton, 1964, pp. 308–314. Rpt. in *Essays on the Language of Literature.* Ed. Seymour Chatman and Samuel R. Levin. Boston: Houghton Mifflin, 1967, pp. 224–230.

Lipski, John M. "Poetic Deviance and Generative Grammar." *PTL* 2 (1977), 241–256.

Miles, Josephine. *Eras and Modes in English Poetry.* Berkeley and Los Angeles: University of California Press, 1957.

Miller, George and Noam Chomsky. "Finitary Models of Language Users." In *Handbook of Mathematical Psychology, II.* Ed. R. D. Luce, R. R. Bush, and E. Galanter. New York: John Wiley & Sons, 1963, pp. 419–491.

Miner, Earl. *Dryden's Poetry.* Bloomington and London: Indiana University Press, 1967.

Ohmann, Richard. *Shaw: The Style and the Man.* Middletown, Conn.: Wesleyan University Press, 1962.

Page, Frederick, ed. *Byron: Poetical Works.* Oxford Standard Authors edn., corr. John Jump. London: Oxford University Press, 1970.

Peck, Walter E. See Ingpen, Roger and Walter E. Peck, eds.

Peterson, R. G. "Critical Calculations: Measure and Symmetry in Literature." *PMLA* 91 (1976), 367–375.

Pope, Alexander. See Butt, John, ed.

Pratt, Mary Louise. *Toward a Speech Act Theory of Discourse.* Bloomington and London: Indiana University Press, 1977.

Putnam, Hilary. *Mathematics, Matter and Method: Philosophical Papers, Volume 1.* Cambridge: Cambridge University Press, 1975.

———. *Mind, Language and Reality: Philosophical Papers, Volume 2.* Cambridge: Cambridge University Press, 1975.

Quennell, Peter. *Byron: A Self-Portrait.* 2 vols. New York: Humanities Press, 1967.

Ramsey, Paul. *The Art of John Dryden.* Lexington: University of Kentucky Press, 1969.

Reichert, John. *Making Sense of Literature.* Chicago and London: University of Chicago Press, 1977.

Reinhart, Tanya. "Patterns, Intuitions, and the Sense of Nonsense." *PTL* 1 (1976), 85–103.

Rorty, Richard. *Philosophy and the Mirror of Nature.* Princeton, N.J.: Princeton University Press, 1979.

Rosenbaum, Peter S. *The Grammar of English Predicate Complement Constructions.* Cambridge: MIT Press, 1967.

Rosenfelt, Deborah Silverton. "Keats and Shelley: A Comparative Study of their Ideas about Poetic Language and Some Patterns of Language Use in their Poetry." Diss. University of California, Los Angeles 1972.

Ross, John R. *Constraints on Variables in Syntax.* Diss. M.I.T. 1967.

———. "Gapping and the Order of Constituents." In *Progress in Linguistics.* Ed. M. Bierwisch and K. E. Heidolph. The Hague: Mouton, 1970.

Searle, John R. "Reiterating the Differences: A Reply to Derrida." *Glyph* 1 (1977), 198–208.

Shelley, Percy Bysshe. See Ingpen, Roger and Walter E. Peck, eds.

Short, Michael H. See Leech, Geoffrey N. and Michael H. Short.

Siegel, Muffy E. A. " 'The Original Crime': John Berryman's Iconic Grammar." *Poetics Today* 2:1a (1980), 163–188.

Smith, Barbara Herrnstein. *On the Margins of Discourse: The Relation of Literature to Language.* Chicago and London: University of Chicago Press, 1978.

Solve, Melvin T. *Shelley: His Theory of Poetry.* Chicago: University of Chicago Press, 1927.

Steinberg, E. R. "Stylistics as a Humanistic Discipline." *Style* 10:1 (1976), 67–78.

Stillings, Justine T. "The Formulation of Gapping in English as Evidence for Variable Types in Syntactic Transformations." *Linguistic Analysis* 1 (1975), 247–273.

———. "Sentence Raising." Bloomington: Indiana University Linguistics Club, 1975.

Stovall, Floyd H. *Desire and Restraint in Shelley.* Durham, N.C.: Duke University Press, 1931.

Swedenberg, H. T., ed. *The Works of John Dryden.* Berkeley and Los Angeles: University of California Press, 1956.

Thorne, James Peter. "Stylistics and Generative Grammars." *Journal of Linguistics* 1 (1965), 49–59. Rpt. in *Linguistics and Literary Style.* Ed. Donald C. Freeman. New York: Holt Rinehart & Winston, 1970, pp. 182–196.

———. "Generative Grammar and Stylistic Analysis." In *New Horizons in Linguistics.* Ed. John Lyons. Harmondsworth: Penguin Books, 1970, pp. 185–197. Rpt. in *Essays in Modern Stylistics.* Ed. Donald C. Freeman. London and New York: Methuen, 1981, pp. 42–52.

Tompkins, Jane P., ed. *Reader-Response Criticism: From Formalism to Post-Structuralism.* Baltimore: The Johns Hopkins University Press, 1980.

Van Doren, Mark. *John Dryden: A Study of his Poetry.* New York: Henry Holt, 1946.

Visser, F. Th. *An Historical Syntax of the English Language.* Leiden: E. J. Brill, 1963.

Weathers, Winston. "The Rhetoric of the Series." In *Teaching Freshman Composition.* Ed. Gary Tate and Edward P. J. Corbett. New York: Oxford University Press, 1967, pp. 313–319.

Whitehall, Harold. "From Linguistics to Criticism." *Kenyon Review* XIII (1951), 710–714.

Williamson, George. "The Rhetorical Pattern of Neo-Classical Wit." *Modern Philology* 33 (1935), 55–81.

Wilson, W. Daniel. "Readers in Texts." *PMLA* 96 (1981), 848–863.

Wordsworth, Jonathan. *The Music of Humanity.* New York and Evanston, Ill.: Harper & Row, 1969.
Wordsworth, William. See Wordsworth, Jonathan.
Ziff, Paul. "On Understanding 'Understanding Utterances.' " In *The Structure of Language: Readings in the Philosophy of Language.* Ed. Jerry A. Fodor and Jerrold J. Katz. Englewood Cliffs, N.J.: Prentice-Hall, 1964, pp. 390–399.

Index of Topics

Adequacy, theoretical, 46–47, 55, 133
Aesthetic factors: role in stylistics
explored, 14, 62, 66, 73, 76, 80, 85–86,
94, 98, 130; defined, 62–66
—pattern: symmetry, 14, 79, 81, 83, 85,
92; defined, 65–66; parallelism, 66–74,
76–77, 83, 87, 90, 116, 119–122, 124; chiasmus, 66, 124–125; concentricity, 66, 77,
79, 81–86, 87, 113–114; mentioned, 67,
77, 81, 84, 85, 86, 87–89, 91, 92, 94, 127
—proportion: distance, 14, 61–62, 64, 65,
91, 92; delay, 59–62, 64, 65, 91, 130; suspension, 60–64, 91; defined, 65; proximity, 91; mentioned, 92, 94
—scale: defined, 65; mentioned, 87–89,
91, 94
Aesthetics, theory of, 63–66, 94, 130
Alliteration, 68, 122
Ambiguity, 7, 31, 40, 73
Anaphoric pronouns: substituting for, 30–
31; mentioned, 71
Argument: traditional methods of, 116;
stylistic, 116–125 *passim*, 128; levels of,
121. *See also* Interpretive strategies,
rhetorical; Propositional argument/
force
Augustanism, 66–67, 73, 86–89, 90, 94,
118, 122, 126–127, 135–136, 147
Author, the, 3, 5, 58. *See also* Poet, the

Biographical criticism, relation to stylistics of, 14, 100, 131

Case grammar, 17
Center-embedding: defined, 39; in poetic
texts, 40, 43, 102–103; mentioned, 60
Characterized reader. *See* Reader, cha-
racterized
Chiasmus. *See* Aesthetic factors, pattern
Cognitive factors: role in linguistic theory
of, 10; as possible basis for syntactic con-
ditions, 39, 43–44, 105
Competence, linguistic, 10–13, 22, 34–35,
60, 76, 77, 86
Competence, literary, 12
Competence, syntactic. *See* Compe-
tence, linguistic
Complementizer, 37
Composition, poetic, 131
Compression. *See* Aesthetic factors, pro-
portion

Concentricity. *See* Aesthetic factors, pattern
Conditions on transformations: role in
linguistic theory, 24, 44; relaxed by
stylists in analyzing poetic language,
28, 34; as evidence of need for cur-
rency of syntactic theory in stylistics,
42. *See also* Index of Syntactic Rules
and Constraints
—violation of, 27, 38, 40, 42, 43–45, 47,
102–105, 107–109
Congruence, structural, 52, 74, 81–82, 86,
119–120, 122
Constraints, syntactic. *See* Conditions on
transformations
Convention, poetic, 87–89, 107–108
Coordinate structure deletions. *See*
Index of Syntactic Rules and Constraints
Couplet, 87. *See also* Heroic couplet, the
Critical theory, goals and standards applicable to stylistics, 3, 76, 100, 101, 108,
131
Cycle. *See* Transformational rules, cycle

Deconstruction, 3–4, 5, 10
Deep structure: defined, 22; proposed for
deviant structures in poetic texts, 48,
53–54, 104; mentioned, 23, 24, 52, 54,
59, 81, 89–90, 112, 114
Delay, 118. *See also* Aesthetic factors, proportion
Derivation, syntactic: defined, 23
Descriptive adequacy. *See* Adequacy,
theoretical
Deviance, syntactic, 17–18, 19, 25, 27–30,
32, 34, 35–36, 44–45, 47–48, 50–56, 73–
74, 76, 102–109, 111, 152
Dialect: study of parallel to stylistic analysis, 13, 56, 129; mentioned, 29, 46, 135
Distance. *See* Aesthetic factors, proportion

Elegies, stylistic analysis of, 2, 59, 107–108,
110
Emphasis. *See* Interpretive strategies,
rhetorical
Evaluating competing critical claims, 99–
100
Evaluative stylistics. *See* Value, literary
Extended Standard Theory (EST): value

Selection restrictions, 22
Semantics: stylistic analysis and, 41, 54–55, 60, 76, 83, 85, 91, 105, 113, 115, 116, 119–122, 124–125; role in linguistic theory, 77; mentioned, 107
Sociolinguistics, parallel field to stylistics, 13
Speech-act theory, 9, 17
Standard language, relation of literary language to, 4–5, 10–11, 12, 13, 19–20, 25, 27–30, 32–35, 38, 40, 41, 44, 45–56, 73–76, 78, 112–113, 135–136, 141. *See also* Deviance, syntactic
Stanza, 87–88
Structuralist grammar, 17, 20, 77
Style: technical aspects of, 13, 14, 15, chap. 2 *passim*, 58–62, 64, 73, 76, 78, 85–86, 94, 98, 102, 106–107, 115, 129–131, 133, 135–136, 138; perceptual aspects of, 14, 15, 18, chap. 3 *passim*, 98, 102, 106–107, 113, 115, 119–122, 124, 127, 130, 133, 138; interpretive aspects of, 14, 15, 18, 64, 65, 77, 80, 84, 86, 90, 93, chap. 4 *passim*, 130–131, 133, 138
—prose. *See* Prose, stylistic analysis of
"Stylistic meaning," 115
Stylistics: goals, 1, 9, 11–13, 14, 17, 29, 96–100, 139; history, 1–7, 9, 45–46, 118, 139; assumptions, 3, 11, 12, 13, 15, 30, 34, 51, 80, 101, 131, 133, 139; methods/methodology, 6, 7, 13, 17–20, 28, 34, 42, 44–48, 55–56, 80, 94, 127, 129; literature in the field of, 9, 15, 17, 65, 113–114, 118; applications to other fields, 9, 58, 66–67, 76, 89, 129, 135–137; terminology, 13, 77, 92, 94, 97, 111, 119, 127–128, 129, 133, 154
—quantitative, 58
Stylistic transformations, 40, 41
Subcategorization, syntactic, 22
Surface structure: defined, 24; association with filters, 24, 27–28; sole location for perceptual stylistic effects, 62, 64, 90; mentioned, 23, 40, 41, 44, 48, 50, 52, 59, 78–79, 81, 90–93, 104–105, 112, 113, 114, 117
Suspension. *See* Aesthetic factors, proportion

Symmetry. *See* Aesthetic factors, pattern
Syntactic competence. *See* Competence, linguistic
Syntax, poetic. *See* Stylistics

Technical stylistics. *See* Style, technical aspects of
Tension: distinguished from suspension, 63–64; mentioned, 2. *See also* Aesthetic factors, proportion
Texts, critical dispute over determinacy of, 3, 5, 7
Traces, syntactic, 144
Transformational cycle. *See* Transformational rules, cycle
Transformational grammar: used in literary analysis of a literary work, 2; general usefulness in literary stylistics, 17, 20–21, 24–25; described, 22–24; great explanatory power of, 24–25, 45; mentioned, 77. *See also* Extended Standard Theory (EST)
Transformational rules: defined, 23; ordering of, 24; cycle, 24; mentioned, 42, 58. *See also* Index of Syntactic Rules and Constraints
—"stylistic." *See* Stylistic transformations
Transformations. *See* Transformational rules
Transparency of surface-/deep-structure relations preferred, 48
Tree structures, 23
Triadic structure as a stylistic device, 67–72, 74, 76, 77, 87, 151

Underlying structure. *See* Deep structure
Ungrammaticality. *See* Deviance, syntactic
Universals, linguistic, 46

Value, literary, 98, 107, 132, 137–138
Violation of syntactic conditions/constraints. *See* Conditions on transformations, violation of

Word-order, role in linguistic theory of, 40–41

Index of Authors

Index of Syntactic Rules and Constraints